I've Been
Everywhere
I'm Going

I've Been Everywhere I'm Going

James G. Mahar

NIMBUS
PUBLISHING LTD

Nimbus Publishing Limited
PO Box 9301, Station A
Halifax, NS B3K 5N5
(902) 455-4286

Cover Design: Arthur B. Carter, Halifax
Printed and bound in Canada

Canadian Cataloguing in Publication Data
Mahar, James G.
I've been everywhere I'm going
ISBN 1-55109-134-8

1. Canadian wit and humor (English) * I. Title.
PS8576.A395I83 1995   C818'.5402   C95-950205-X
PR9199.3.M34I83 1995

Contents

Chapter 1
The Sad Thing About Writing Humour

*"There are many different kinds of writing,
but only one is difficult—humour."*
Mark Twain

A few years ago my wife and I were at a Tony Bennett concert and during the program, as this very talented man sang his repertoire of popular music, I thought, "This guy has it made! He can sing the same songs over and over, night after night, and the audience loves it. In fact, if he didn't sing 'I Left My Heart in San Francisco' and 'Rags to Riches,' the people would demand it." The same goes for dancers and instrumentalists. They rarely have to learn anything new. They dance the same steps, play the same numbers, do the same routines, and this is perfectly acceptable.

But, pity the poor humorist. He can't tell the same joke or story twice. One of my favourite stories has always been the one about the compulsive gambler named George. This man would bet on anything, anywhere, anytime. At his funeral, during the church service, the minister said, "George is not really dead—he merely sleeps." One of George's buddies, also an inveterate gambler, who was seated at the back of the church, leaped to his feet and yelled, "Oh yeah! Well I've got a hundred bucks that says he's really dead." I used that story in a column a few months ago; it's gone forever so I can't tell it to you now.

Not only can the humorist not tell the same story twice,

there's an awesome list of subjects that he or she can't joke about, not even once. Take drunk driving for example. I just simply can't tell you about the drunk who was going ninety miles per hour the wrong way on a one-way street because he felt a moral obligation to get home as fast as he could—before he had an accident. This isn't funny because drunk driving is no longer socially acceptable, and rightly so.

Making fun of someone's home town or country is also not done today. You might get away with it if you gave the place a fictional name, Hoohooland for example. Then if you were having a glass of wine with a few friends some night, you could gaze thoughtfully at your glass and say, "Does anyone know the favourite wine in Hoohooland?" When they admit they don't, you can hit them with, "The favourite 'whine' in Hoohooland is, 'Why doesn't the federal government do something to help us?'" This is a nice play on the homonym, whine/wine, but I won't use it because, with my luck, there really will be a place named Hoohooland and most of the residents thereof will be in the audience—I could get hurt. The comedian of today can't use ethnic jokes, religious jokes or minority jokes. He or she cannot tell stories about doctors, mothers-in-law, women drivers and a host of other groups without being inundated with nasty letters. And if you're fool enough to crack wise about banks, lawyers or tax departments, nasty letters will be the least of your problems—they'll getcha. There's hardly a subject that's not offensive to someone.

Personally, having a real weird and irreverent sense of humour, my favourite category has always been sick jokes. Like the one about the young boy who had his left foot run over by the ten-tonne asphalt spreader. He is recovering nicely in room 202 at the hospital. His left foot is also recovering—in rooms 202, 204 and 206. He has a terrible time finding jogging shoes that fit.

But if I can't tell you that one, then wild horses couldn't persuade me to tell the one about the lady who was making funeral arrangements for her deceased husband. She said to the undertaker, "My husband wore a hairpiece and this was always a source of embarrassment to him. None of his friends knew about it, and I would like you to make sure it's firmly in place for the viewing." The undertaker assured her it would be taken care of. A few days after the funeral the woman came to pay the costs and she said, "I realize that you may have gone to extra trouble with the hairpiece but I was well pleased with the service, and if you need to charge me a little extra, I would find that acceptable." The undertaker said, "No madam, that's quite all right; the original price quoted will be sufficient—after all, what could I possibly charge you for a half-dozen two-inch nails?"

Now that you haven't read these stories that I can't tell you, perhaps you should read the stories I can. Hopefully you will find them inoffensive and good clean fun. Today, almost every field of medicine is taking humour very seriously because there is general agreement on the therapeutic value of laughter in reducing stress and pain. Chuckling oxygenates the blood, pumps up the aerobic level, gives a workout to the cardio and respiratory systems and just plain makes you feel good about yourself and the world around you. It's a drug-free high. It has been stated that a hundred lusty guffaws burn the same amount of calories as a ten-minute workout on a rowing machine.

Please turn the page to start your new fitness program.

Chapter 2
Little Louie the Logger

As bad as the recent recession has been, it does not compare in severity with the Great Depression of the early thirties. The best way to compare the two would be to say, in a recession everyone must tighten their belt; in a depression you don't have a belt, and a lot of people don't even have pants.

It was during the Great Depression that Louie read the newspaper ad that said, "Logger wanted for local lumber camp; only the best need apply." In those days employers were picky—millions were out of work and only the very best, or a close relative of the boss, had any chance of finding work. Come to think of it, that's not much different from today!

Louie was a proud man. He did not like being on relief and accepting charity. This job could solve the problem. The pay was good, the food was plentiful and he didn't doubt his ability, he had been taught by an expert. In a glow of optimism Louie packed a few belongings in an old, battered suitcase and headed for the woods.

He arrived at the lumber camp about noon the next day, just as the loggers were filing out of the cookhouse. There were ten of them. All of them looked to be as strong as an ox—and several looked to be almost as clever. They were huge men. Louie felt almost insignificant, but gamely he introduced himself and told them he was applying for the job. This caused spasms of hilarious laughter and oodles of smart remarks.

"Hey, that's great. We can call you 'Little Louie the Logger,' " said one, which wasn't fair; Louie was five feet and eight inches and weighed about 150 pounds, which was pretty average.

Another said, "Boy, I eat more for breakfast than you weigh, what makes you think you could be a logger?"

In the midst of their derision, Louie emptied the contents of his wallet—four one dollar bills—and said, "This is every cent that I have. I'll bet this and my suitcase and contents that I can chop down any tree faster than the best man you've got." The gauntlet had been flung!

These were not the type of men to refuse a challenge. "All right, Little Louie, you're on," said the foreman. "We'll get big Pierre to teach you a lesson."

They picked two trees about one hundred feet apart. Both were about the same height, both were a foot in diameter. Louie looked at his tree, picked up his suitcase and walked about thirty feet away. He laid the suitcase down, stood up, measured the tree again by eye, bent down one more time and adjusted the suitcase a few inches closer to the tree and an inch or so to the left. Again he eyed the tree and nodded affirmatively—that was about right.

When both Louie and Pierre were ready the foreman yelled, "Go!" Pierre lifted his axe and took a mighty swipe that sank the blade deep into the trunk of the tree. But then a miraculous thing happened; Little Louie became a blur. The staccato thwack of his axe became a continuous roar. Bits and pieces of tree flew like confetti, showering the staring spectators. Before Pierre could make a decent dent, Louie's tree gave an anguished crack and began to fall. Slowly at first and then with a mighty rush it hit the ground, bounced once and settled. The very top of the tree touched the very centre of the handle of Louie's suitcase.

There was silence. Ten loggers, with a combined height

of 62 ft. 7 1/2 in., and a total weight of 2,844 lbs., stood stunned into absolute silence. It was the silence that follows a performance of such magnificence it cannot be rewarded by mere applause. It was the silence that would have followed the parting of the Red Sea, the multiplication of the loaves and fishes, the changing of water to wine.

The foreman was the first to break it. "Good Lord! Where in the name of all that's holy did you learn to cut trees?"

With a gentle smile Louie replied, "I worked with my father when he had the contract to clear-cut the Sahara Forest."

"Sahara Forest? There's no Sahara Forest—there is only the Sahara Desert!" said the foreman.

Modestly, Louie replied, "Sure ... NOW!"

Chapter 3
Do You Accept Cash?

I first noticed the little girl when she cracked both of my ankles with the shopping cart. I'm very observant, I always notice things like that right away. I was going to have a chat with her mother about it, but her mother was glaring at me with a look on her face that said, "You clumsy oaf, how dare you get in my daughter's way?"

So, I said nothing. I did keep an eye on the kid while I limped around getting my groceries, wondering if the supermarket provided courtesy wheelchairs. Later, when she wiped out a floor to ceiling display of canned milk, I was two aisles away and there was no way they could blame me for that. The resulting horrendous crash, the screams of nearby customers and the rattle of the rolling cans got the attention of the store manager, and he came out from wherever store managers hide when they are not dealing with catastrophes.

With a remarkable display of control that I could only envy and certainly never emulate, he curled his lips back from his clenched teeth in what could loosely be described as a smile. He walked over to the candy counter, picked up an all-day sucker and handed it to the little girl. She snatched it from his hand like a starving chicken-hawk clutching a wounded sparrow.

I think the manager's intention was twofold. First, he wanted to assure the lady there were no hard feelings. Just because her adorable little tyke had destroyed a display that had taken three employees all day to build; just because the crash had dented 163 cans of milk they now could not sell; and, just because it would take an hour during the busiest time of the day to clean up the mess—he is not upset. See—he is smiling—would he be smiling if he was upset? Second, I think he was trying to get the little darling's mind off destroying the Fruit and Vegetable Department, which he believed was next on her hit list.

The mother does not seem to be upset about the mess, in fact, it appears that she could not care less. She is slightly embarrassed by her daughter's behaviour. In a stern voice she said, "Bratilla, where are your manners?"

Bratilla—what an appropriate name. I could see the BRAT part right away; it took a few seconds to grasp the connection to ATILLA. I didn't see that until her mother called her 'Hon.' The mother persisted, "Bratilla, you know better. What does mommy always say when someone gives her something nice?" Bratilla, the hon, finally sensing what was expected of her, removed the sucker long enough to scream, "CHARGE IT."

They are learning at an early age that credit buying makes the world go round. If it were not for credit cards, stores would only sell a fraction of the things they do now. Manufacturers would cut back on production. There would be mass lay-offs. Credit card companies would go out of business; banks would have to be content with exorbitant instead of astronomical profits. Taxes would increase to support the people who are out of work; there would be soup kitchens and food banks and the whole country would be in a terrible mess.

Come to think of it, the country is in a terrible mess now—with credit cards—but that's another story.

Credit cards have many advantages: they eliminate the need to carry large sums of money; they keep an accurate record of all the things you shouldn't have bought; they help you to get into a financial mess you could never achieve if you had to pay cash; and they prevent you from getting too much sleep by keeping you awake at night worrying about how to pay them.

The only disadvantage is they lull you into a false sense of bonhomie that cons you into buying things you don't need with money you haven't got to impress people you don't like.

Because of this last statement, weak-willed people like me cannot afford to have credit cards. We are those pathetic creatures at the end of a long line of card holders. We are the ones who, when we reach the cashier, lower our eyes in embarrassment, shove a handful of twenty dollar bills in the direction of the cash register and mutter, "I'm awfully sorry, I don't have a credit card. Do you accept cash?"

Chapter 4
I've Been Everywhere I'm Going

If I had been the navigator for Christopher Columbus, we would all still be Europeans. I have a terrible time with maps. In the first place, I just don't trust them and there is a good reason for this. If you look at a map of North America you'll notice that they show the United States as being green and Canada as being red, and this is just simply not true. I've flown over both countries and Canada is definitely not red; the lakes are blue, the forests are green and the mountains are brown with some white on the tops. The United States is much the same, in fact, from ten thousand feet you can't tell one from the other.

If they're going to lie to you about something as basic as this, think of what other misinformation these maps could contain. Not only do you have to contend with misinformation but whoever makes these things insists on making them upside-down. Everywhere I'm leaving from is at the top of the map and everywhere I'm going to is at the bottom; this means I have to turn the stupid thing the other way around. Try reading those little upside-down names on a jiggling map while hurtling down a freeway at seventy or eighty miles an hour on a dark night and you'll see the problem. To make it worse, I don't have my glasses on; I can barely see the huge transport truck that is five feet ahead of my front bumper.

Information that should be on a map is never there. For example, one stormy night I was whistling through a small town. It wasn't much of a town; just a couple of houses and a bridge. According to the sign on the bridge it was a little place called, SLIPPERY WHEN WET. It wasn't on the map but it should have been. My car skidded and went out of control, and hazards like that should be noted on the map. After all, it's the responsibility of those people to make driving as safe and pleasant as possible for the motoring public.

Asking directions from people is not much better. I remember one time I stopped and asked an old fellow who was leaning on his fence how to get to a certain place. He gave me some complicated directions that I followed to the letter, and about thirty minutes later I arrived back where I started. Same old guy, same old fence. When I asked him how come, he said he was just making sure I knew how to follow instructions. I asked him where the tourist bureau was—he didn't know. I asked him where the post office was—he didn't know. In exasperation I said, "Buddy, you don't know very much do you?" He said, "Maybe not, sonny, but I ain't lost." This was a very unkind remark. I've never been lost. Occasionally I've been confused for a day or so, but never lost.

The least confusing way to travel is by light aircraft. All you have to do is take off, go up to about three thousand feet and follow the railway tracks. If you're in any doubt about where you are, come down to a few feet above the tracks and zoom past the railway station; they all have the town name on them.

Incidentally, this livens up most small towns; since your plane has pontoons for landing on water, they figure you must be crashing. Everybody races around in their cars with camcorders stuck out the windows trying to get some video tape they can sell to the evening newscast. Meantime I have my camcorder out the window recording the head-on collisions, pedestrians being flattened, and assorted fender-benders. Unfortunately, in one such place, a little town named, according to the sign on the railway

station, 'noskateboardinganytime' (probably Welsh) some yahoo took down the call numbers on the plane and called the authorities. They revoked my regular pilot's licence and issued a conditional licence. The condition is I'm only allowed to fly over the Sahara Desert, and then, only from midnight to 5 a.m. on Sundays.

The other night, when my wife and I were getting ready for bed, I said, "I'm a bit hungry, how about a sandwich?" and she said, "I'm exhausted, how about going down to the kitchen and making a sandwich for yourself?" I went downstairs and wandered around for awhile, through the living room and dining room and then to the rumpus room and finally back up to the bedroom. I woke her up and said, "Okay, so how do I get to the kitchen from here? And keep it simple."

Chapter 5
Physical Fitness After Fifty

I had a friend who was an absolute nut on fitness. He jogged, lifted weights, did push-ups and sit-ups and bought every new piece of equipment that promised to increase his level of fitness. He was dedicated to strenuous sports. During the winter season he went skiing once every six weeks. He would have gone every day if he could but it took six weeks to get the cast off whatever bones he broke the last time. In the summer he was devoted to every sport involving a ball, which was unfortunate because he had the coordination of a mortally wounded water buffalo. He looked ridiculous missing every ball by a foot or two but the splendid conditioning that he had attained allowed him to look ridiculous all day without even being out of breath. Unfortunately, at age thirty-two, he jogged into the path of a gravel truck and was instantly killed. That's the bad news. The good news is that the coroner said my friend was the healthiest corpse he had ever examined.

A few weeks before the accident he said to me, with a supercilious smirk, "You must be close to seventy and you look to be in great shape; what fitness program do you follow?" Thoughtfully I replied, "The best plan is to get up about six in the morning, do an hour of push-ups, sit-ups, and deep knee bends, then either run two miles or briskly walk five miles. For the rest of the day, carefully watch what you eat, make sure you get a well-balanced, nutritious diet from the four basic food groups—no junk food—no cigarettes—no alcohol, and get eight hours sleep every night. I call it 'JIM'S PHYSICAL FITNESS AFTER FIFTY, SYSTEM ONE.' "

He looked at me with new respect and asked, "How long have you been doing that?" I said, "I'm thinking of starting first thing tomorrow morning."

Actually, I'm not. You would have to be some kind of an idiot to go through a program of physical torture like that first thing in the morning, and I'm certainly not your average idiot! Besides, it's too expensive! Ben Gay Ointment alone runs to about six hundred dollars a year! Add to that the cost of prescription pain killers for the shin splints, muscle spasms and lower back pain, and I just can't afford it. There is very little chance that it will make me live longer; it's only going to seem longer.

There have been hundreds of fitness programs advanced over the last few decades, and every week somebody, somewhere, comes up with an idiotic new one. There are newspaper and television ads for video tapes by some of Hollywood's glamorous personalities that assure you that, in the privacy of your own home, by following their workout tape, you can lose weight and be as slim and trim and gorgeous as they are. Don't you believe it! The reason they look so good is that they make so much money selling those stupid tapes, they can afford to spend a fortune on plastic surgery, liposuction and tummy tucks. But you aren't going to look any better; you're just going to look exhausted, and the only weight you are going to lose is from your wallet.

Before you jump to the conclusion that I'm opposed to all physical fitness programs, let me assure you that I'm not. There are two systems that appeal to my common sense. The first is the "GEORGE BURNS FIVE MARTINI WORKOUT." In this, you simply drink five dry martinis, smoke a dozen cigars and run around with beautiful, young ladies in their early twenties. Before you snicker in derision, may I point out that it certainly works for George! Unfortunately, I can only adopt part of this program. I don't mind the dry martinis and I can stand the cigars, but my wife won't let me run around with beautiful, young ladies in their early twenties. In fact, she doesn't allow me to run around with any ladies of any age, beautiful or otherwise.

To supplement George's program, I've added some exercises from another program that I also admire. This additional program was designed by watching our cats. My wife loves cats, dogs, horses and me—not necessarily in that order—so we have seven cats. It's amazing how much you can learn from them. When they're young they're very frisky. (When I was young, so was I.) As they mature they seem to get most of their exercise from prowling around all night chasing members of the opposite sex (no comment), but as they grow older they develop a very sensible program that I call "THE FELINE FITNESS FORMULA."

When they awake, they yawn and stretch. Just once— no repetitions. For the rest of the day, they eat when they are hungry, sleep when they are tired and make an earnest effort not to stand in the rain. That's it. No jogging—even with four legs to evenly distribute the shin-splints, they never jog. They don't lift weights—the heaviest thing I've ever seen a cat lift is a mouthful of tuna. They still play a little bit from time to time (so do I) but nothing very strenuous.

There are a few things that cats do that I would not recommend. I wouldn't try scratching the back of my head with my foot. (I can do it—but it gives me a terrible headache); and don't curl up into a complete ball with your paws over your head when you're sleeping; you'll probably injure your back. Slithering through the shrubs sneaking up on a sparrow is also sort of silly. If you want to

eat grasshoppers and swat at butterflies, that's up to you -
it's optional on this program.

However, a combination of the "FELINE FITNESS
FORMULA" and the "GEORGE BURNS FIVE MARTINI WORKOUT"
provides us with the ultimate fitness program. I call it "JIM'S
PHYSICAL FITNESS AFTER FIFTY, SYSTEM TWO."

The first thing you must do, in system two, is forget all
that stupid stuff you were told in system one. This makes
most people feel better instantly. When you awake, yawn
and stretch—once—no repetitions. For the rest of the day
you simply eat when you are hungry, drink five dry
martinis, sleep when you're tired, play a little if you feel
like it (nothing strenuous), smoke a dozen cigars, have
some catnip from time to time and try not to stand in the
rain. If you don't like catnip, try a nice wine.

I must warn you—on a well-designed, physical fitness
program such as this, you are bound to wake up some
mornings feeling so good that you have an urge to leap out
of bed and do something stupid like running a couple of
miles or mowing the lawn or something equally ridiculous.
Don't do it! Stifle this urge! Roll over and go back to sleep
until it wears off!

Someday, with practice, you may work up to the ten
martini level and then, even if you're not in good shape—
who cares!

Chapter 6
Proverbs for Pessimists

I once had the misfortune to work with a pessimist for a period of two months. That was enough! Those were the longest, most discouraging two months of my entire life. No matter what we were doing, no matter how well it was going, he knew it would turn sour. And even if it did turn out okay, then something else was sure to go wrong—he just knew it. Sure enough, when this guy was around, you could count on things going wrong. He inspired disaster. He could turn certain victory into stunning defeat; there wasn't a parade he couldn't rain on. This type of person has the power to brighten everyone's day just by not showing up.

I'm the exact opposite; I am now, always have been and hopefully always will be an optimist. Whenever a difficulty arises, I tell myself that 'EVERY CLOUD HAS A SILVER LINING' and 'IT'S ALWAYS DARKEST BEFORE THE DAWN.' When I embark on any project I remember 'WELL BEGUN IS HALF DONE,' 'AN OAK IS NOT FELLED AT ONE STROKE' and 'A JOB WORTH DOING IS WORTH DOING WELL'; and, if things go wrong, 'IF AT FIRST YOU DON'T SUCCEED, TRY, TRY AGAIN.'

During my formative years I was bombarded with slogans and proverbs. We were in the midst of the Great Depression of the thirties and people grasped the ray of hope that was offered by these little gems of optimism. 'WHILE THERE IS LIFE THERE IS HOPE,' 'WHERE THERE IS A WILL THERE'S A WAY,' and 'ALL COMES TO HE WHO WAITS' suggested that better days were just around the corner.

There was little tolerance for waste. If I heard it once, I heard it a million times, 'MONEY DOES NOT GROW ON TREES,' 'WASTE NOT WANT NOT.' These were usually tacked on to a five-minute lecture about times being desperate, how lucky I was that my father had a job despite his cut in salary, and I should eat everything on my plate whether I liked it or not. If I did leave food on my plate, I heard 'HUNGER IS THE BEST SAUCE,' if you don't eat it now, maybe it will taste better tomorrow.

Some proverbs I had trouble with. 'THE EARLY BIRD CATCHES THE WORM.' I felt sorry for the worm. What good did getting up early do him (or her)? 'SAVE SOMETHING FOR A RAINY DAY.' As far as I could see, we didn't have anything to save, and days couldn't get any rainier than this!

Whenever I tried, 'KEEP YOUR EYE ON THE BALL, YOUR EAR TO THE GROUND, YOUR SHOULDER TO THE WHEEL, AND YOUR NOSE TO THE GRINDSTONE,' I wound up with a pinched nerve in my neck and lower back muscle spasms. I used to hate 'ACCIDENTS WILL HAPPEN IN THE BEST OF FAMILIES' because they all turned and stared at me.

Some I found unworkable. 'DO UNTO OTHERS AS YOU WOULD HAVE THEM DO UNTO YOU' never worked out, so I changed it to 'DO UNTO OTHERS BEFORE THEY DO UNTO YOU.'

Toward the end of the Depression, I made up some proverbs of my own. 'YOU CAN LEAD A HORSE TO WATER, BUT YOU CAN'T MAKE HIM GROW MOSS' was my favourite. And then there was 'A FOOL AND HIS MONEY ARE SOME PARTY' and 'ALL WORK AND NO PLAY MAKES JACK AND PLENTY OF IT.' If someone started in about how terrible times were and how rough they were having it, I would solemnly declare, 'IF WE HAD SOME HAM, WE COULD HAVE SOME HAM AND EGGS IF WE HAD SOME EGGS' or 'IF THINGS DON'T ALTER, THEY WILL STAY AS THEY ARE.'

Only recently it has occurred to me that most proverbs are aimed at creating optimism. I feel that this is unfair.

After all, pessimists are people, too, and they don't deserve to be discriminated against! So, for those of you who embrace pessimism, I'd like to offer the following proverbs:

1. EVERY SILVER LINING HAS A CLOUD.
2. A JOB WELL STARTED IS BOUND TO FOUL UP.
3. IF AT FIRST YOU DON'T SUCCEED, QUIT.
4. AFTER THE STORM COMES THE FLOOD.
5. IF YOU WANT A THING WELL DONE, GET SOMEBODY ELSE TO DO IT.
6. GOD HELPS THOSE WHO GET CAUGHT HELPING THEMSELVES —ON CLOSED-CIRCUIT SECURITY CAMERAS.
7. WHERE DOES IT GET YOU—IN THE END ?

Adhering to these little gems of philosophy will enable you to maintain an attitude of doom and gloom—even in the best of times.

Chapter 7
That's Show Biz

As Jimmy Durante often said, "Everybody wants to get into the act." Witness the number of people who will pay an outrageous price to have their hearing impaired by the latest heavy-metal group, or are willing to suffer a nauseous attack of vertigo during a laser light show. People will stand by the hour watching a magician perform. Oblivious to their surroundings, their single thought is, "Where in the name of Heaven did the dove come from?" (I'll tell you later.) Almost everyone fantasizes about performing before an adoring audience. Most people will never have their dreams come true.

My own career in show business began one April night in 1938 at exactly 8:00 P.M. It ended that same night at precisely 8:03 P.M. It was a school play entitled "The Hound Howled at Midnight"—a murder mystery. I wasn't part of the original cast. The boy who was to play the part of the victim did not show up and I was a last minute substitute. They told me it would be simple. All I had to do was lie quietly on the stage and pretend I was a dead body during act one. Since I just happened to have a body, was notorious for my ability to lie down and was already considered brain-dead by many of the teachers, this did not seem to place undue strain on my thespian talents. I was wrong. At the command, "Places everyone," I lay face down with my head almost touching the curtain. I heard the curtain go up, and the French maid, the cute girl from Grade 10B, entered from stage left. She dusted some of the furniture, rearranged some flowers and then discovered my body. She leaned over me and let go one horrendous, shrill scream right in my left ear. Nobody told me she was going to scream. If a hound had howled, I would have expected that. As it was, I leaped about a foot off the stage, propped myself on my elbows and yelled, "Geez!" Within a few seconds I had transformed a murder mystery into a comedy. They should have called it "The Audience Howled at 8:03." They rang the curtain down, waited ten minutes and tried again. The second time was much smoother; after all, I'd had a chance to rehearse.

Back to the dove. Years later, because no one, anywhere, ever, would consider casting me in a play, I decided to promote a few shows of my own. One of the entertainers I hired was a magician named Ron. Over the years we became good friends, and I accepted an invitation to visit with him and his wife for a week during December. It was a working holiday. Ron was doing four shows a day and I acted as an assistant. One of my jobs was looking after the doves. This is a very docile bird ideally suited to a magician's act. Before the show, the dove is encased in a black pouch equipped with snap fasteners; attached to the pouch is a stiff, black wire with a finger loop. The black pouch is in a black, slant pocket in a black coat that is over a black vest. You can't see it. To make the dove appear, Ron would hook his finger in the loop, haul the pouch up behind the silk scarf he was changing from blue to yellow (I'll tell you how that is done another time.) and open the pouch. Voila! A dove!

This worked smoothly until the final night when the doves decided to make it a memorable evening for me. Instead of staying where they were put, two doves flew up to a rod on the back wall of the stage. At Ron's prompting, I entered stage left with a twelve-foot ladder—mild applause. The first dove was easy but the second was slightly out of reach. Locking my legs around the ladder I stretched out; and, just as I got the dove, the ladder flipped over—tumultuous applause! Now I'm pinned between the ladder and the wall with a dove clutched in each hand. The ladder and I slither slowly and majestically down the wall—standing ovation!

Later, Ron said this was a class act and we should make it part of the show. But no way. I'm not wasting comedic talent like this on a magic show; I'll see if Red Skelton needs a partner—or George Burns or maybe I'll write some funny stories—or something.

Chapter 8
The Handy Woman

Whenever any of our friends call to speak to my wife, they always say, "Hello, Jim, is Rowena handy?" And my stock answer is, "No, but I'm going to keep her anyhow; she looks good in front of the fireplace on cold winter nights." This whole statement is false. We don't have a fireplace and my wife's extremely handy. Take the time we came home late at night and found that we were locked out. Her keys were in her other purse upstairs, and I'd lost mine. She sticks a hairpin in the alarm system switch, wiggles it a few times and the red light goes out. Three thousand dollars worth of the most modern, sophisticated, electronic motion sensors and infrared detectors have been bypassed. The same hairpin unlocks the 100 per cent burglar-proof, tamper-proof, no-home-can-afford-to-be-without-this-type-of-exterior-door-lock lock. Elapsed time 9.3 seconds. I throw away the rock I was about to smash the front window with and follow her into the house.

I have a complete set of power tools and hand tools that are the best that money can buy; with these I'm totally inept. She has her hairpins, a thin dime she uses for a screwdriver and a carving knife with the tip broken off. With these, and a great deal of ingenuity, she can fix anything from a stopped-up sink to the latest IBM software. She knows the precise spot to kick on the TV to stop the picture from tumbling. To start the dishwasher, it has to be thumped to the left of the switch with the handle of her broken carving knife. To the left, not the right; the carving knife, not my screwdriver. The sequence of these rituals is important.

One Saturday morning I awoke feeling on top of the world. I felt like leaping out of bed and really doing a good day's work around the house. Normally, when I awake feeling like this, I roll over and go back to sleep until it wears off. But this particular day I got up. After a quick breakfast I went down to the basement to get the tools I would need: twelve sheets of three different grades of sandpaper, my electric plane, an assortment of Phillips and Robertson screwdrivers, and a two-foot steel square. When I arrived upstairs with this load of equipment my wife said, "What do you intend doing?" I laid the tools carefully on the kitchen counter, in the middle of the tea biscuits she was preparing and said, "I'm going to fix that dining-room door that scrapes on the floor. First I have to take it off the pin hinges, then I have to lay it on the dining-room table. Next I have to mark a quarter of an inch on the bottom with the steel square, plane it with the electric planer and sand it with the sandpaper. After that I have to set it back on the pin hinges—probably will take me all day." She removed the dough from under the electric planer, "Oh, good! For a moment there, when I saw all those tools, I thought maybe you were going to build a replica of the Taj Mahal."

She took one sheet of coarse sandpaper, laid it on the floor where the door was jamming, and moved the door back and forth a few times over the sandpaper. Voila! The door's fixed! Elapsed time 5.5 seconds. She said, "Don't bring the mountain to Mohammed, bring Mohammed to the mountain." Whatever that means.

Over the years I've learned to have complete faith in her ability to fix things. Regardless of how silly her methods might appear, I've been conditioned to follow them religiously, without question. So when my new power saw refused to start, I called upstairs to her, "My new power saw won't start." Her answer, "Change your shoes." Well, it sounded stupid to me but I walked upstairs from the basement, through the kitchen hallway and upstairs to the bedroom. I kicked off the black oxfords I'd been wearing and selected the brown suede pair with the silver buckles. Thus equipped, I made the return trip to the basement and switched the saw on again. Nothing. She missed. At last she's failed. Gloatingly I went back upstairs, "You're wrong; I changed my shoes and it still doesn't work." She looked at me with a puzzled frown, "Your shoes? What the hell do your shoes have to do with the power supply? I said 'Change the fuse.' " Perhaps I should've rolled over and went back to sleep after all.

Chapter 9

The Rowing Machine

My wife bought me a rowing machine for my birthday. It was delivered on Thursday and placed in the middle of the living-room floor. There it stayed for several days while I occasionally walked past it at a discreet distance and examined it with a wary eye. The warmth of feeling I have for exercise machines falls only slightly above that which I have for black mambas, great white sharks and enraged pit bulls. Under the title, "Rowing Machine," in smaller letters, it says "another fine product of the HARI KARI CORPORATION, HIROSHIMA, JAPAN." The name Japan does not unduly bother me, after all they make some good stuff and their reputation for craftsmanship is respected throughout the world. But HARI KARI and HIROSHIMA do little to generate enthusiasm.

I must admit I am slightly intrigued by the picture on the carton. This is of a young man, sitting on the rowing machine, obviously having the time of his life. Dressed in a pair of very short shorts, a soggy sweatband just beneath his luxurious curls, he is a glowing picture of buoyant good health. Every muscle is bulging. He is smiling a beatific smile of supreme joy and contentment, and I don't blame him one bit. If I had a body like that I, too, would wear a beatific smile. My opinion of the contraption improves slightly. Perhaps it's worth a try.

After all, I am the first to admit that I am a tad overweight. For those of you who are not familiar with the ancient Babylonian system of weights and measures, one

Tad is equal to 15.7 kilograms. For those of you who are not familiar with the metric system, I can't help you; neither am I.

I unpack the various bits and pieces and arrange them in a semi-circle around the box. I immediately see the first problem—the size of the carton. Mandrake the Magician couldn't get all of those bits and pieces back in that small a box. I suspect that somewhere in Japan, hidden from view, there is a factory devoted to the production of boxes too small for anything to fit. Next to it is another factory, staffed by highly skilled crammers, who figure out how to do the impossible.

These two factories, working together, have saved Japanese industry zillions of yen in returned merchandise each year. Since the sales slip clearly states, in five languages, that any return must be in the original carton, I'm stuck. No wonder their economy is booming. Japanese ingenuity has triumphed again!

Later that evening I decided to assemble the thing so I could have a better look at it. Now, whenever I assemble anything, the first thing I do is throw away the instructions. I find that following explicit instructions takes the sporting element out of anything. It destroys that thrill of discovery, that feeling of joy that comes from finding any two pieces that fit together without the use of a hammer. I did glance at them for a moment, long enough to note that the HARI KARI people are assuring me that a ten-year-old child can completely assemble this equipment in five minutes. Where I'm supposed to find a ten-year-old Japanese kid this time of night they don't say.

After three hours, two skinned knuckles and a sprained wrist, I went next door and got my neighbour's ten-year-old kid out of bed. He's not Japanese but, by now, I'm not in the mood to quibble about race, creed, or colour. Well, it took him seven minutes and thirty-two seconds, but that was probably because he was still half asleep. With a supercilious smirk he informed me it was not nearly as difficult as the exercise bike that he assembled for me last year. I hate that kid! Next year, when he is eleven and has outlived his usefulness, he's going to be in big trouble.

Now comes the moment of truth. It's time to test drive the thing. I put on the new jogging suit that she bought me for my birthday last year and sit down on the seat. Problem number two is the seat. I suspect that at the HARI KARI FACTORY, when the ten-year-old kid is not busy assembling things, they get him to sit in a tub of wet clay. This becomes the mold for rowing machine seats. There is absolutely no compatibility between their seat and mine. Their seat is too small and made of hard plastic; mine is much larger and made of a much softer material. Theirs was shaped by a ten-year-old rump; mine was shaped by too many years of the good life—pizza, beer, french fries, etc. I try a pillow.

Now I'm up too high. The oars are chipping little pieces of bone off my kneecaps. What's the use of having a perfect body if you can't stand up? But, with the dogged determination for which I am famous, I stick with it. On the eighth stroke I get a stabbing pain across my shoulders. Being one of those whose threshold of pain is not only very low—it's practically non-existent—my distress is immediately apparent to even a casual observer. My wife is far from being a casual observer. She is tuned in to every little quirk of my devious nature. "What's the matter now?"

Bravely I replied, "Oh, it's nothing; just a sudden pain in my back—and chest." Why I added chest, I don't know.

"Well, stop immediately. Men your age are dying like flies every day. Go upstairs right away and lie down; I'll come up in a few minutes and massage your back." Since this is the best offer I've had all day, I readily comply.

The moment I take off the jogging suit I discover the cause of the stabbing pain. I forgot to remove the pins. I'm not about to tell her this. There are some things it is better for wives not to know. I yell downstairs, "How about a shot of bourbon to relax my muscles?" There is no answer. Perhaps she is remembering the night a few weeks ago when, after a few shots of bourbon, my muscles were so relaxed I couldn't stand up. It was worth a try.

It's amazing how a strenuous physical workout stimulates the brain. As I lie here half asleep waiting for my massage, images flit through my mind—rippling muscles, Japanese kids, swooning women, men my age being swatted like flies. It's wonderful to have a wife who gives you presents that can make these dreams come true. I hope that next birthday she gets me that weight-lifting outfit I was looking at in the sports store. The picture of the guy on that box makes the guy on the rowing machine look like an anemic wimp.

Chapter 10

I See by the Paper

Last night I read the following item in the evening paper:

TOILET READY FOR ROOF OF THE WORLD
GLASGOW, SCOTLAND (Reuter)
British scientists preparing to climb Mount Everest
today were given their first glimpse of a toilet
designed for use on the roof of the world. The steel
cubicle, equipped with steel guy ropes anchored
with ice picks to prevent it being blown off the
mountain, has a wooden seat, as plastic would be
cold to the touch and would crack in the freezing
temperatures. A Scottish firm designed the toilet,
which cost about $14,850. It is to be taken by
Sherpas up the mountain in seven pieces.

This completely spoiled the rest of the evening for me.
In fact, I didn't even read the rest of the paper, I just threw
it on the floor and sat there and brooded all night. The
article is too sketchy, there is much it doesn't say, and my
mind boggled at the possibilities. For example, it says that
the toilet is ready for the roof of the world—it doesn't say if
the roof of the world is ready for a toilet! How much
pedestrian traffic do they plan on having up there?

Even if there are a lot of people planning on visiting the
most remote spot on earth, and even if they can get
permission from the Government of Tibet, would it be too
much to expect for them to go to the bathroom before they
start? If they plan on waiting until they climb about five

and a half miles, practically straight up, they may well be too late by the time they get there.

Since this contraption is being constructed by a Scottish firm, it is not beyond the realm of possibility that it will be a pay-toilet. So, what happens if whoever climbs the 29,028 feet discovers that he or she left all their change in their other pants or purse at the base of the mountain. Don't laugh—it would be far from funny.

Since we just considered he's and she's, how come only one toilet? Shouldn't there be at least two, one marked 'MEN' and one marked 'LADIES'? I hope they don't identify them with those stupid silhouettes. I always have trouble, I can't tell if it's a man, or a woman wearing slacks; and the one of a woman I confuse with a guy wearing a kilt. This leads to a great deal of embarrassment on my part and a great deal of high-pitched screaming on theirs.

If we are going to have two, we might as well go all the way and have a family washroom with diaper changing facilities. Although anyone who wants to drag a kid up the side of Mount Everest to change a diaper is out of their skull—most parents don't seem to be able to make it the length of a mall.

Years ago, before Mount Everest was first climbed by Edmund Hillary, it was considered to be the most pristine place on earth. Untouched by pollution or the invasion of mankind, it was a symbol of chastity. Hundreds had tried to despoil it, many died in the attempt and are still there. But, in the same manner as beating the four-minute mile, once one did it, everyone got into the act.

From photographs that I have seen, the level portion of the top of Mount Everest is hardly bigger than my patio, but now it is littered with the flags of a dozen nations, four coke bottles, assorted empty beer cans, two ham sandwich wrappers, an assortment of ice picks, and dozens of cigarette butts. (It is the only place on earth that does not have a non-smoking section—yet.)

Who do you think will get stuck with the job of cleaning this toilet? Knowing the British from my years in the R.A.F., I can safely bet a bundle it will be the Sherpas. This is not going to tickle them pink. They consider Mount Everest a goddess, a sacred mountain, and having a British outhouse stuck on top of it will not fill them with joy. In fact, they will probably cut the guy wires and let the whole contraption take off in the breeze. If someone happens to be in there—tough bananas.

If nothing else, we will have to change some music. We now know, "How High the Moon" (29,028 feet), but a slight change is needed for "I'm Sitting on Top of the World."

Chapter 11
Don't Diet—Erase It

Every week I buy about four of the tabloids. Now, if anyone asks me, I tell them I buy them because my wife reads them. Although that's true, I must admit I also browse through one or two from time to time. What grabs my interest in these papers are the headlines. Most of the headlines are concerning weight loss, personalities, or the Royal Family. In very large print you read things like "I LOST 38 LBS. WITH THE WONDER DIET PILL—AND YOU CAN, TOO" or "LOSE 15 LBS. IN ONE WEEK WITH THREE NEW CRASH DIETS." Sometimes, to add impact, they combine diet headlines to personalities—"HOW OPRAH LOST 26 LBS.—AND NO ONE NOTICED." The ultimate is when they combine weight loss and the Royal Family—"CHARLES LOST 131 LBS. IN ONE DAY— DI WALKED OUT."

When I read these headlines, I think of my Uncle Milton and the skill, ingenuity, and diligence he used to invent a system of losing weight without any dieting whatsoever and absolutely no exercising. Except for one minor flaw it would probably be in use worldwide today.

I don't actually remember Uncle Milton too well; he disappeared when I was very young. But I certainly heard about him. Everyone in our family, my parents and all my relatives, were in awe of this man. With great pride they would tell me what a genius he was and how he came up with invention after invention in many fields. I don't think that I ever sat down to a dinner that included mashed potatoes that I didn't hear how Uncle Milton crossed the ordinary potato with a sponge and produced the super potato that's grown in many countries today.

Frankly, I never really thought they tasted all that great, but they held over seven times more gravy than any other potato, if you like lots of gravy I guess that's really something to be happy about.

It was in the field of transportation that he excelled. In the early 1900s he turned his talent to building better and safer ships; and, it was he, and he alone, who was responsible for the design of the watertight compartments that made the Titanic unsinkable! Years later he collaborated with his cousin 'Smoky' to produce the complicated and highly sophisticated fire control system eventually used on the Hindenburg.

When he turned his marvellous, inventive genius loose on the problem of dietless weight control, he came up with the same awe-inspiring results. Milton had a great fondness for peanut butter fudge and chocolate-coated anything. When his sweet tooth kicked in and propelled him into a frantic fudge binge, he'd gain two or three pounds in a week. He wasn't the type of person who could tolerate the deprivation and sacrifice of dieting; and he could never stand even the thought of physical exercise. So, he simply applied that splendid brain to the goal of constructing a simple, mechanical method of ridding himself of excess pounds.

They say he just sat in his workshop for three days, without sleep, and stared at the eraser on his pencil, while munching on a large bowl of peanut butter fudge. Then followed two months of hectic days and sleepless nights. Ideas were tried, discarded, adapted, modified. There were days of elation and enthusiasm followed by weeks of gloom and despair. And then the big breakthrough—success at last! Uncle Milton had fashioned a queen-size, rubber mattress that fitted perfectly on his bed. This mattress had the same consistency and properties as the pencil eraser. Now, as he lay in bed at night, in the comfort of his own home, without dieting or exercise, he lost weight. The normal rolling over and twitching around erased those unwanted extra pounds. Sometimes, in an extremely restless night, he'd erase too much and the next day he'd have to pig-out on potato chips and beer—but this wasn't a problem. Basically, Milton stayed the same weight for years and indulged in all the goodies he could eat.

Then disaster struck! The furnace cut out on a cold January night while he was in a really deep sleep; and, for the rest of the night, he shivered and shook in the freezing cold. In the morning Milton was gone—all they ever found was his wristwatch strap. On the death certificate the cause of death was listed as "ACUTE ERASERITIS," but none of the family thought there was anything cute about it.

Uncle Milton's gone now—as I said, he disappeared when I was quite young. But his memory lingers on. To this day, I can't eat peanut butter fudge or stare at an eraser without thinking of Uncle Milton.

Chapter 12
Happy Birthday to Me

If I told them once, I must have told them a dozen times, "Don't light all the candles." The fire marshal, a man who should be respected as an authority on the subject, told them, "Don't light all the candles." Even the people in the burn unit at the hospital, and they should know, called and said, "This year, for heaven's sake, don't light all the candles!" So, what did they do, they lit all the candles! There are seventy of them this year.

Before they even get the thing to the living room, they've set fire to three people in the kitchen, scorched the ceiling tiles in the hall and activated every smoke alarm in the house.

And what am I supposed to do with it after it's placed in front of me? You can't even look at the thing without wearing at least two pair of really dark sunglasses; and the heat is unbearable! Even moving my chair back four feet from the table, I can smell my eyebrows scorching. There's no way I can blow those candles out! I won't be getting my new teeth for another two weeks. If you want to really make some funny noises, try blowing out seventy candles with no teeth.

Fortunately, my wife is equal to the situation. She has experienced the same thing with every birthday I've had since the sixty-fifth. Earlier in the day, with great foresight, she brought the garden hose in through the living-room window. A couple of quick squirts and the problem is solved. An added benefit—the cake is now very moist; I hate a dry birthday cake.

A birthday is an ideal opportunity for sober reflection. Well, reflection at least, it doesn't necessarily have to be sober. It's a chance to look back at what might have been, should have been and what really was. To look back from this distance, I need binoculars or maybe even a telescope. But, I can still see myself as a twelve-year-old, trudging from the library every Saturday with a pile of books about doctors and medicine. I wanted to be a brain surgeon. By the time I was sixteen I realized this was not to be. I have a proclivity to hiccups. There is nothing messier than fooling around in somebody's brain with a really sharp knife when you have the hiccups.

Many people who flunk brain surgery become plumbers. The pay is about the same, or slightly better, and it is not nearly as hazardous to the patient. But I couldn't do this because I can never remember which is the hot end of a soldering iron—and that can really smart if you are wrong.

Then World War II started and I decided I would be a fighter pilot. What could be more glamorous than that? Picture me, the devil-may-care hero of a hundred aerial combats, on leave, strolling down Piccadilly Circus in my well-worn, medal-bedecked uniform, a gorgeous, adoring female on each arm. This dream didn't fly either. It seems fighter pilots need good eyesight; and, without my glasses, I'm as blind as a bat. I tried to bluff my way through the eye-test. When they said, "Can you read the bottom line on the chart?" I gave an enthusiastic, "Certainly, the bottom line is 'MADE IN U.S.A., PATENT NUMBER 8974732149.' " It didn't work. I did serve in the air force, but no aerial combat, no glamour, no femlae companions.

It has been the story of my life. Nothing that I planned on worked out or came to be. But that's all right. Somebody up there likes me. The things I've done over the years have been more enjoyable than anything I could have planned. From day one I've had a ball. I still plan things I would like to do but if they don't pan out it doesn't matter, I know something better is just around the corner.

Now that I'm seventy I'm even starting to become mellow. Just last week I smashed my thumb with the hammer and very softly I said, "Good heavens, I do believe I have smitten my lovely thumb with the beautiful hammer." This is a far cry from my language pattern of a few years ago, developed during my years of service with the R.A.F.

Well, my next birthday is over eleven months away but it's not to early too start planning. I think I'd better tell them not to light all the candles.

Chapter 13
Long After the Stupid Beep

Since time began people have been inventing things. It started when someone chipped a piece of flint and made a spear. With this we were more than a match for some dumb brute that was twice our size, especially that big dumb brute in the next cave. Flint was replaced with copper and copper by iron; spears were replaced by bows and arrows, in turn replaced by guns and nuclear bombs. Today, thanks to ingenuity, instead of killing things one at a time with spears, we can push a button and kill millions. We've come a long way.

While some were working on spears and stuff, others developed the wheel. Somebody else invented an all-weather tire and anti-lock brakes, and before you knew it, we had gridlocks and traffic jams. A distance it would take you almost an hour to walk in the old days, you can now do in about three hours in the comfort of your car. The inventive potential of the human mind is awesome.

Eventually, when the fields of killing and transportation were well under control, the inventors turned to the wonderful world of communication. Today we have computers and modems, fax machines and cellular phones and a host of other devices that bring joy and frustration to our everyday lives. I have all these modern gadgets and I don't think I could get along without them, but the one piece of equipment that really annoys me is the telephone answering machine.

Oh, sure, when they first came out, I thought they were

great. I said to myself, if either one of my friends call and I'm not here, they will leave a message and I'll call them the minute I get back. Not so. Nobody leaves a message. The worst part—everyone I call also has one of the fool things and I never get to speak to anyone any more. I do hear lots of interesting stuff on their machines. I can listen to W. C. Fields mumbling at me, or an invitation by Mae West to "come up and see her sometime," or their cute little four-year-old reciting "Mary had a little lamb"—but no way do I get to talk to the person I called. The usefulness of this equipment has been distorted by the public.

I suppose the most blatant misuse that I know of happened last winter to a friend of mine. Milton had been told, many times, he needed either a new furnace or extensive repairs to the one he had but he was the world's worst procrastinator and did nothing about it. One bitterly cold night in early February, when the temperature dropped to twenty below zero, the furnace finally blew and set fire to the stuff stored in the basement. My friend had been sitting in the kitchen addressing the envelopes to mail last year's Christmas cards (I told you he was a procrastinator) and he handled the situation very calmly. He's a pretty cool customer. Without undue panic he went to the basement, shut off the oil supply and sprayed the flames with the fire extinguisher.

Unfortunately, the fire extinguisher ran out of gook before the basement ran out of fire. By now the room was full of heavy, dense smoke and noxious fumes and Milton beat a hasty retreat back to the kitchen. He picked up the phone, dialled the fire department and this is what he got:

"Hi there! Thank you for calling your local fire department, we appreciate your patronage. All of our firemen are busy at the moment and we cannot answer your call in person.

"If you are calling from a touch tone phone and the fire is a fat-fire, please press one ... if the fire is electrical, please press two ... if the fire is of other origin, please stay on the line and, after the beep, give your name and address, your phone number and fax number, your social insurance number, a brief description of your fire and the location of the nearest fire hydrant. Please, stay calm. As soon as we have the firemen and equipment available, your conflagration will be extinguished with the utmost speed and efficiency. Meanwhile, we strongly suggest you remove yourself from the premises before you get your butt burnt. Don't forget to grab your insurance policy on the way out. Remember, we are here to serve you. Thank you for calling, keep the home fires burning, have a really nice day, and here is the beep."

Chapter 14
Pity Poor Willie

Last night I spent a quiet evening reading the story of Romeo and Juliet, by William Shakespeare. That must have been at least the twelfth time I've read that story, but it never fails to grab me. For a few hours I am lost in a world that is oblivious to phone calls or interruption. That particular story always creates a sweet, sad ache in my heart. The pathos of their young, pure love, pitted against the unrelenting hatred of their families always makes me wish I could have helped those poor, unfortunate lovers. At heart, I'm a romantic type.

As heart-stirring as the story might be, what impresses me even more is the brilliant word-pictures painted by this master craftsman. One moment his lilting words have the soft whisper of love and dreams—moments later the urgency of fire and passion. Turn a few pages and words alone convey the intense, vicious hatred of Capulet for Montague; the hideous clash and clang of swordplay; the anguish of death and shattered lives. Shakespeare's artful vocabulary clutches and explores your every emotion, compelling you to enter the world of his characters, feel their joys and pain, rejoice with them, grieve with them. Never before or since has an author so masterfully displayed this power. The story of Romeo and Juliet has been 'borrowed' by thousands, but none have surpassed the brilliance of the original. None ever will.

After I finished the story, I put the book down and sat there a long time thinking about William Shakespeare. I thought about the man and his writings; and, with a shock, it struck me that at least ninety per cent of the words he used are either obsolete or have changed meaning.

I thought about the famous balcony scene when Juliet says, "Wherefore art thou, Romeo." She doesn't mean 'Where are you?' She means 'Why are you.' In her soliloquy she is bemoaning the fact that she has fallen in love with Romeo Montague. If his name had been Herbert Finklestein or Roger Shagnasty, they could have been married and had children or had children and got married, whichever. She could have taken him home to her folks and everything would have been A-okay. As it was, Romeo is the sworn enemy of her family; if she takes him home, stuff will hit the fan. If she had meant 'where' she would have said 'whither,' like in 'whither goest thou?' So whither means where and wherefore means why. Wherefore this is I know not. If Willie were alive today, not only would he be 431 years old, he would be practically illiterate. He would be a fumbling bumpkin. He couldn't fill out an application for a driver's licence—although why he would want to at his age escapes me. The man who was the most prolific writer of all time would be speechless—almost every word he knew is gone.

Another thought struck me. How could he possibly write all that stuff? He didn't even have a computer. A computer! He didn't even have a ballpoint pen, for gawdsake. He plucked a plume from a turkey or whatever, dipped it in a jug of ink and scribbled on a piece of parchment. What way is that to write stuff? I'm having enough trouble writing this, and I have an enhanced keyboard, 428 megabyte hard drive, windows, DOS, WordPerfect, spell-checker, grammar-checker and a 24-pin dot matrix printer. The only turkey is the one sitting at the enhanced keyboard.

Even after he had something written—how does it get

from there to the publisher? He didn't have a fax machine or a fax/modem on the computer he didn't have. How are you supposed to send stuff if you don't have a fax machine? There weren't any telephones, telegraph, postal service or courier. There wasn't radio or television or satellite dishes or fibre optic cables—there wasn't much of anything. All he had was the kid down the street that delivered things when he wasn't busy practising fencing and jousting.

One thing he did have was an unbelievable amount of talent, and when you have that you don't need the enhanced keyboard, 428 megabyte hard drive, windows, DOS, WordPerfect, spell-checker, grammar-checker and all that other jazz. Maybe I'm making much ado about nothing. Hey! Much Ado About Nothing—that would make a great title for a play. I'm going to run out and see if I can find a turkey.

Chapter 15
The Small One

We live in a world of constant change and the pace of change is accelerating at an alarming rate. Years ago it took a decade or so for something to become obsolete. Now it happens within a year, sometimes less—sometimes much less. Your new computer and most electronic equipment is outmoded the moment you buy it. By the time you master the latest software, they introduce a new version; the beautiful record collection you spent years compiling is negated by the invention of compact discs.

So be it. I have no quarrel with advances that bring improvement—we could use a great deal more of it; what I do object to is change for the sake of change—we could use a great deal less of that.

Over the years there are many products that I have used consistently and these products have attained the status of friend. I know exactly what they can do and how they do it; I know what they cannot do and why. Therefore, a chill goes through me when I ask for one of my old friends and the store clerk tells me, "Oh! That's the old 793XE6. We don't stock that model any more. We now have the 204GL5. It's better and it's guaranteed for forty years."

With that, he plonks it down on the counter with the proud expression of a mother displaying her new born babe. I can't understand his proprietary attitude. He didn't invent it, he didn't manufacture it, he doesn't even know how to use it. All he did was take it out of the carton and put it on the shelf. He has done away with my friend and is offering me a total stranger as a substitute.

The forty year guarantee also leaves me cold. This company has been in business less than a year. According to the Department of Statistics, a company starting up today has a fifteen per cent chance of still being in business five years from now, and only three per cent of those will still be in business in twenty years.

This gives them about one chance in two hundred of being around to honour the guarantee, they have to be either optimists or idiots. I assume the latter. "Son, I am not guaranteed for forty years. Frankly, my chances of making it to 108 years of age are not all that great. However, they are about twenty times better that your chance of still being in business when I get there. Now I'll give you a guarantee: If I do make it, and you are still in business, and if there is anything wrong with this product, I'll be back—count on it."

Another area of change for the sake of change is the supermarket. Almost every package, bottle and can displays a label that says "NEW AND IMPROVED" in very large letters. It makes you wonder what kind of no-good garbage they were palming off on us last year. I like to take one of those products to the nearest clerk and say, "So, what was wrong with it?" They usually look shocked and stammer, "What do you mean?"

I point to the "NEW AND IMPROVED" and say, "Obviously if it is improved now, then there must have been something wrong with it before—what was it?" They mumble something about asking the manager and wander away. They never come back.

While I'm on the subject of supermarkets, one of the things that really bothers me is the liberty they take with the language. Take sizes for example. Once there was small, medium and large. Nothing could be more simple.

You knew what was what.

But they couldn't leave that alone, they had to change it to large, economy and giant family size. I don't know about you, but I picture a giant family as a ten-foot-six Mommy and an eleven-foot-eight Daddy, who have two delightful little tykes who are eight-feet-three-inches. Sometimes, if I'm in a playful mood—which I usually am, and I can get a clerk's attention—which I usually can't—I will take one of the packages that says 'LARGE' and say to him, "I would like to have a small one of this."

He looks at the package and says, "That is the small size."

I say, "No it isn't, this is the large one. See, right there in block letters it says LARGE—L-A-R-G-E."

He says, "Yeah, but you see the large one is really the small one."

With a puzzled frown, I say, "Son, how can that be? Small and large are comparative terms; for something to be the large then there must be something of the same nature that is smaller, and conversely, if something is smaller than another size it cannot be the large because, clearly, it is smaller than the large size. It could be medium. There is always that possibility. But for it to be medium there must be a size that is smaller than it and another that is larger than it or there is no medium for it to be. The medium one would have to be larger than the small one but not as large as the large one, but I don't want the medium one and I don't want the large one—I want the small one. For you to say that this is the small one is in direct contradiction to the manufacturer, who clearly states that this is the large one—see, right there in block letters—LARGE—L-A-R-G-E. So, therefore if this is the large one, and the manufacturer says it is, and they should know, after all they make the stuff, then by logic there has to be at least one size that is smaller, and maybe even two sizes that are smaller, one of which would then become the medium, assuming that it is larger than the small but smaller than the large. So where is it or they or them or whatever?"

By now he is sweating and the aisle is jammed with carts and the people near me are trying to explain what is going on to the people further back. "I'll try to explain" he says. "We call the small one the large one because it's smaller than the other two sizes, which are the economy and the giant family, but you can't call the giant family size the large size because you are already calling the small one the large one. So, even though the biggest one is the largest you can't call it the large one if you are already calling the small one the large one, okay?"

It's starting to sound like an Abbot and Costello routine and everyone, including me is thoroughly confused. "Look son, let's just forget it, okay? I don't really like the stuff anyhow. I think I'd rather go buy some grapes—do you know if they have any large grapes?"

Chapter 16
The Letter—Or, How to Ruin Your Wife's Vacation

Some wives think that husbands are helpless idiots when it comes to doing housework. They seem to think that there is some mysterious talent needed to make the beds, dust the furniture, prepare the meals and clean the house, and only they possess it. Nothing could be further from the truth.

While it may be true that some men are helpless idiots, I am one that is far from being helpless. I am competent in many fields, and I see no reason why housekeeping should be beyond me. I had a chance to prove this last summer when my wife decided that she would like to spend a month visiting her childhood home.

She left on Sunday afternoon. I'm free! The first week was wonderful! No one picking up after me—no one losing my place in the books that are piled around my lazy-boy chair, hanging up my clothes where I can't find them, putting things back in their proper place where I'd never think to look. Everything I need is here on the floor beside me. Is that efficiency or what?

By Friday I have the house organized. The living room is my control centre. Normally she is not too fussy about me being in the living room; she says I clash with the drapes. If she could see the way I've organized it, she would be really impressed. I've piled the clean clothes on chairs—socks on one, shirts on another, underwear on a third—everything in plain sight, easy to get at. The dirty clothes are piled on top of and around the washer. Unread books are on one side of my chair, the ones I've read on the other. The dirty mugs, beer glasses and dishes are on top of the magazines that are on top of the newspapers that are on top of the television. This separation of clean, dirty, read and unread eliminates confusion.

Another area that needs efficiency is making the beds. I always got the impression from my wife that making the bed was something that requires a B.A., a Ph.D., and years of experience; not so. There is actually nothing to it. When you get up in the morning, you throw the covers back; when you go to bed at night, you haul them back over you. Where's the big deal? I will admit that by Wednesday it is getting kind of rumpled and messy but that's no problem. Move over to the other bed; and, when that gets the same way, there is the spare bed in the other room plus two perfectly good sleeping bags. You have to plan ahead.

Meals are another area in which I have been misled. I have seen my wife spend three or four hours preparing a delicious meal of roast beef, baked potatoes, vegetables, and Yorkshire pudding followed by chocolate mousse and coffee. There is no need of this. I can make a peanut butter and jelly sandwich in less than a minute. (It helps if you leave the knife stuck permanently in the peanut butter jar—no messy clean-up.) You simply eat peanut butter and jelly sandwiches until you get sick of them. Then, since a good diet demands variety, you switch over to cheese sandwiches until you feel like eating peanut butter and jelly sandwiches again.

Dusting is the only thing that I found a bit baffling. By the time you dust the last piece of furniture, the first piece needs it again. The dust just sort of hovers around for a while and then settles again. Very frustrating. I tried conning my next door neighbour's wife into doing it for me. I told her that I could write my name on any piece of furniture in the house but all I got was a snort of derision and a cool "Ain't education wonderful! Those six years you spent in grade five have finally paid off!"

No help there.

By the time she has been gone for a week, the house doesn't have that pine-fresh scent anymore. It is more the aroma of a dead water buffalo that has been lying under a tropical sun too long. Maybe I should clean up the rotten cat food in the kitchen. All three sinks are full of dirty dishes—the two in the kitchen and the one in the bathroom. The house seems to be full of flies. I opened the front door to let some of them go out, but none seemed so inclined. As a matter of fact, a few of their relatives and friends came in. I piled some of the dishes in the bathtub. I thought maybe they would get washed when I took a shower but I kicked them over and smashed them. It's tough taking a shower with a lot of broken glass under your feet; you have to wear boots. I suppose it could be worse. At least I'm not stupid enough to sit in the tub for a bath.

By now I am willing to concede there may be more to keeping house than is apparent to most husbands. This place has reached the point where drastic measures are called for. As I see it, I only have two alternatives. I can apply to the government to have this house declared a disaster area and get federal aid to clean it up, or I can con my wife into coming home. The first alternative takes months. The second only takes 'THE LETTER,' and the results are almost instantaneous. I will write the letter:

Hi Sweetheart!

Well, here it is a week since you left. If anyone deserves a vacation it's you. You just relax and have a good rest. Don't worry about anything here; everything is going great. I've followed your instructions faithfully since you've been gone. Every morning I put a fresh bowl of milk and a dish of cat food on the kitchen floor for your cat. In fact, there are six bowls of milk and six dishes of cat food there right now. Half of them have gone rotten. I haven't seen your cat since last Monday but he probably will come home when he gets hungry. Don't worry about it, relax and enjoy yourself.

I have some good news and some great news for you. The good news is the insurance company is going to pay half of the smoke and water damage. They would have paid the whole thing but they figure half of it is my own fault for throwing water on the burning fat. The great news is the hole the firemen chopped in the kitchen wall is in the exact position where you always wanted a picture window. How about that! Is that luck or what?

I'm having a contractor drop in tomorrow and give me a price on enlarging it, framing it and putting in the glass. Don't worry about cost. I accidentally found the money you had hidden in the envelope marked 'Personal' that was in the pillow case under the photo album behind the clothes in the bottom drawer of your dresser. I'll use that.

Love, Jim

P.S. Why would your collection of African Violets turn brown? How do you turn the burglar alarm off? It doesn't bother me; I keep the tape deck cranked up so loud I don't hear it, but some of the neighbours are starting to get nasty.

Chapter 17
Stock Answers

I'm really a very lazy sort of person. I always take the path of least resistance. This is never more apparent than in the conversations I have with people. To eliminate a lot of wear and tear on my brain I have, over the years, developed a lot of stock answers that require no thought on my part. These quick answers pop out under the stimuli of standard questions or situations. Being a humorist, I try to keep them funny.

Just after New Year's Day I met a friend and asked him how he had spent New Year's Eve. He said, "We didn't go anywhere this year. We decided to just stay home, relax and take it easy." This called for one of my stock answers. "I know what you mean. After the spectacle my wife and I made of ourselves last New Year's Eve, nobody invited us anywhere, either."

Years ago my wife and I spent a lot of money and time learning ballroom dancing. This is really a fun thing and we enjoyed every moment. At a dance, since most people never bothered with lessons, we looked very competent and graceful and invariably someone would comment on our ability. A gentleman, standing next to me at the bar, might say something like, "Man, if I could dance like you I would be on the floor for every single number." Stock answer: "Sir, if you think I look good, next time keep an eye on my wife. She is wearing a long, tight dress and she's doing everything I'm doing; and, what's more, she's doing it backwards while wearing spike heels. Now that really takes talent."

Sometimes I am telephoned by someone, generally a few minutes before I'm about to go to dinner, and they want me to do something for them that is going to take four hours of hard work. When I ask them when they need this they usually say, "I have to have it by one o'clock." This, of course, is impossible. Why they leave it so late to order the thing, I will never know. I could give them a lecture on the evils of procrastination, but I prefer to hit them with a stock answer, "I'm very sorry, you have the wrong number, you should have dialled Rescue 911, they are the only people who move that fast."

Stock answers come in handy even when visiting people in hospital. You aren't going to have a chance to say much—they are going to monopolize the conversation with a long tale of woe about the ailment or injury that put them there. So whatever you do say had better be good. If you wait patiently, until they wind down, you may get the chance to put in your stock answer. For example, a man who worked for me, named Mel, was in hospital after triple-bypass heart surgery. Now this is pretty drastic stuff and Mel was one of the first people to ever have this type of operation. This heart operation went to his head and he couldn't stop talking about it. He was in intensive care for over a week, and it was a least three or four days after that before he was allowed visitors. I was the first one.

Mel looked absolutely terrible. His complexion was chalky-white; his eyes were glazed with pain. There were tubes sticking in him and an equal number sticking out; electronic probes were taped to his chest, and an assortment of bottles on a stand beside him were making ominous, gurgling sounds. I've seen many dead people who looked far healthier than Mel.

For a half-hour I couldn't get a word in while he related all the grim, gory details of everything the doctors had done to him and the intense, unbelievable pain he had suffered. Finally, from sheer exhaustion, he stopped talking for a minute. Now was my chance. In a concerned tone of voice I said, "Mel, I know what you are going through, I'm no stranger to pain." Leaning toward him I held out my index finger. "You see that finger, well just last week I had a hangnail that was absolute agony, it must have hurt for at least an hour."

It is better not to do this unless the patient is near death's door or has two broken legs. There is nothing more embarrassing than having someone in a johnny-shirt chasing you down a hospital corridor dragging a stand full of gurgling bottles.

Chapter 18
Unclutter Your Life

A friend of mine claims there are only three types of people. According to him there are people who are Irish, people who wish they were Irish and another group composed of poor, ignorant heathens. Personally, I feel this is an oversimplification that is somewhat influenced by the fact that his name is Michael Patrick O'Flaherty. Although I don't believe O'Flaherty's grouping of the world's six billion people is accurate, I do believe that most of us can be categorized into two groups: those who never throw anything away; and those who get rid of everything they don't immediately need.

For most of my life I have belonged to the first group. I didn't realize how much junk I've kept until one Saturday morning a few weeks ago when I said to my wife, "I used to have a red fountain pen that was a joy to write with, you haven't seen it anywhere have you?" She thought about it for a moment and then said, "No, but it may be in that carton with your Boer War souvenirs." This was sarcasm, of course—I don't go back that far.

Well, I finally found it about six hours later and unfortunately it doesn't work anymore. It was in one of the cartons with my World War II souvenirs. To find it I had to move a whole pile of useless junk. There was the old dishwasher they don't make parts for anymore, the old kitchen range that used to blow all the fuses, three electric razors and an assortment of small appliances, all hopelessly broken—fourteen cartons of old newspapers and magazines that have articles in them that I intend writing something about someday (maybe), and that stupid oil painting of the bunch of weeds.

Why I bought that I'll never know. I found it in a junk shop years ago and paid eight bucks for it. It's hideous, really garish colours, and it looks like it was painted by someone demented. All these years it was behind a pile of other junk—but no more. I put it in a garbage bag, carried it out to the curb and left it for garbage collection. That was the only thing I got rid of right away. The rest I piled in the middle of the basement floor. After about a week my wife complained because she had to climb over it to get to the washer and dryer. I told her there was too much for me to carry, so I was having a man with a truck come in next week and cart it all away.

I'm so enthused by the success of my cleaning-out efforts that I think I will pass on some basic rules to help you avoid the pitfalls of clutter:

1. Whatever it is, if you haven't needed it in the last six months, give it away. Let someone else store it, you'll be surprised at how much more room you have in the basement;

2. Never keep anything white—it will get dirty and you will wind up cleaning it;

3. Wear a blindfold when you are cleaning out old newspapers and magazines or you're going to waste the afternoon reading last year's comic strips and articles you intend writing something about, someday, maybe;

4. If your closets are getting full, sort out some of the clothes and send them to the Salvation Army—preferably some stuff belonging to your spouse;

5. Above all, get rid of anything that has become useless. (Husband/wife excepted.)

Last night my wife was reading the paper and she said, "It says here that some old homeless man out at the landfill site found an oil painting that everyone thought was lost forever. It's called *Wildweeds* and it was painted by Vincent van Gogh a year before he died. They say it could be worth as much as thirty million." She looked at me and said, "There are some real idiots in this world, can you imagine anyone stupid enough to throw away a valuable painting like that?"

Saturday I think I'll rearrange the stuff in the basement. Maybe I'll put up some shelves for more storage space. Instead of getting rid of things, maybe I should just organize it better. What I really need is a good filing system. If I had a good marker pen I could list the contents on the cartons, I think I have one, somewhere, it was a nice blue one—I'll ask my wife where it is.

Chapter 19
Weird Pets

It's not that I don't like animals. To the contrary, I love cats and dogs and I have been known to pat a horse occasionally. It's just that I think there are some creatures that shouldn't live in the same place as people. Take boa constrictors, for example. Some people have these snakes in their home and consider them a wonderful, easy-to-care-for pet; and, I suppose, in a way, they are. They don't have to be fed very often. If they swallow your cat or the neighbour's dog or a small child or two, you don't have to feed them again for weeks. This saves running around opening cans of pet food and changing litter pans all the time, and I guess that's good.

But I'm the type of person who likes to sit quietly at night and read a book or watch the violence on television. I don't need violence in my living room. I don't mind a cat curling up on my lap for a good snooze, and if a dog wants to sit alongside of me, I'll pat it. What I do mind is some creature dangling from the chandelier and considering me as a six-month supply of high energy protein. I don't want to get into a wrestling match with a household pet.

I think I know more about snakes than most people. During World War II, I was in the air force and served in West Africa for a year and a half. I saw lots of boa constrictors, and I never met one that I liked. The biggest one I saw was over twenty feet long and it started to slither towards me. Everything in Africa that crept, crawled or slithered, did it towards me! I turned and ran down the runway. I don't know how fast I was going but there was a Wellington bomber taking off at the same time and I passed it with ease. If I had held my arms straight out for lift, I probably would have been at ten thousand feet before the bomber!

I didn't mind those things outdoors where I have room to run but we had one in the billet as a pet. He was only eight feet long, a baby, but it disturbed me. When I get up in the middle of the night, I find it disconcerting to step on a snake! How do I know it's 'our' snake! Maybe it's a poisonous type like a black mamba, or a pit viper or whatever. Everyone said, "Don't worry about it—it keeps the rats away. No rat is going to stay in a billet that has a boa constrictor." Well, this airman wasn't either—I moved.

The move wasn't that much better. The new billet had a pet chimp named Charlie. This was the filthiest creature I ever slept in the same room with, and there's been some dandies. He knew absolutely nothing about personal hygiene. He used to sit on the spare bunk by the hour and jam sticks of gum in his mouth and smoke cigarettes. Everyone else thought it was cute. I thought it was disgusting.

Every day, when I was stepping out in the boiling sun and the 125°F heat to spend the day crawling around in scalding hot aircraft, he'd stretch out on the bunk, under a fan, eating bananas and listening to the radio. He'd curl his upper and lower lips back and reveal his tobacco-stained fangs and laugh in derision. This arrogant chimp actually thought he was smarter than people! He disappeared into the jungle one day and never came back. Good riddance! I hope something really vicious got him.

The weirdest pet I ever met was Ozzie. Ozzie was a six-foot, 350-pound gorilla. He and his owner, Calvin, used to go to the movies every Saturday night in a little town in the South of England. The townspeople didn't get upset;

they were used to Ozzie. In fact, they liked Ozzie more than they liked Calvin. One night, during the movie *Gone with the Wind*, a stranger came in and sat down alongside of Ozzie after the lights were out. He didn't seem to notice Ozzie was a gorilla. Maybe he thought it was just some big guy with a smelly fur coat. The stack of bananas on Ozzie's lap should have tipped him off—everyone else had popcorn. When the lights came up, the guy went ape! He leaped about ten feet away and screamed, "You can't bring a gorilla to a movie like this!"

Calvin very calmly said, "Why not? He loved the book—and he has a definite crush on Scarlet O'Hara."

Chapter 20
Jogging is for the Birds

Many years ago I had a friend who was an avid disciple of jogging. In fair weather or foul, in driving rain or howling blizzard, in tropical heat or fifty below zero temperature, he just had to jog his five miles every day; and, he couldn't keep quiet about it. He just had to spread the gospel of fitness among all his friends. If he told me once, he told me a thousand times that if I were to jog it would add ten years to my life. Eventually he wore me down and I did try it. One night, after dark, I went to the track at a sports centre and jogged a hundred yards. He was right! At the end of the hundred yards I felt ten years older; I barely made it home! That one time cured me.

This jogging craze began when someone started the ugly rumour that the average thirty-year-old North American was in about the same physical condition as the average seventy-five-year-old Swedish grandmother, or words to that effect. This, of course, is absolute nonsense. When I was thirty years old, there were not too many seventy-five-year-old Swedish grandmothers that I could not beat in a fair fight. Nevertheless, the general public believed this outrageous statement.

This lie was compounded by the doctor who wrote two books extolling the benefits of jogging. In those books, he outlined various jogging programs that would strengthen the heart and lungs and improve the muscle tone, coordination and general well being of participants. He was regarded as the ultimate authority on the benefits of jogging. His arguments were well presented, and he would probably have expanded on them in additional books had he survived the heart attack he died from—while jogging.

But this misinformation triggered an excess of frenzied activity that has now reached ridiculous proportions. Everybody is out jogging. Well, everybody except me. I hold the firm belief that if God had intended us to be joggers, we would all have been born with three diagonal stripes on the sides of our feet. We were not. Furthermore, if there is a benevolent God, and I truly believe there is, and He expected us to jog, which I truly believe He didn't, He would not have created beings who have a proclivity to sprained ankles, shin splints, twisted kneecaps and arthritic hip joints—not to mention lower back pain and muscle spasms. At the moment of creation, He would have been stingy with the use of bone, muscles and tendons and lavish with titanium, stainless steel and reinforced plastic. It's obvious to me He did not intend our frail, human forms to contend with the shock, strain and stress of jogging.

Jogging is not a happy pastime. You have but to listen. Joggers produce a cacophony of harsh, disagreeable, unpleasant sounds. They gasp, huff, snort and puff. They wheeze, whine, rattle, gurgle and grunt. These are far removed from the accepted sounds of pleasure. The 'AAHHH' that follows the first sip of a cool beer on a hot Sunday afternoon is a sound of pleasure. The 'MMMM' that follows the first mouthful of a delicious strawberry shortcake smothered in whipped cream is a sound of pleasure. But the sounds produced by joggers are those associated with pain and strain. They are not happy.

Have you ever seen a jogger smile? I never have. Oh, they do have one expression you might mistake for a smile—that's the one where the lips are curled back from the teeth. But this is the grimace of pain beyond pain. It is not a smile.

But I'll tell you who does smile. The manufacturers, wholesalers and retailers who sell all the gear that joggers seem to think they must have—that's who. The people who make jogging suits, head bands, wrist bands, ankle weights, stop watches ad infinitum, all smile. The pharmacists who supply the ointment for sore, aching muscles, the hot water bottles, ice packs, over-the-counter and prescription pain killers not only smile, they chortle with glee. And the people who make jogging shoes go into paroxysms of hearty great guffaws. There must be a zillion kinds of shoes out there. They have walking shoes, running shoes, shoes for running uphill, shoes for running downhill and even special shoes to wear while you are running around looking for your other shoes. Most joggers get most of their exercise just changing shoes. And now, they have the ultimate. For only $145 you can buy a pair that has an air-pump built in. When I asked why, they said you pumped them up to get a snug fit. Personally, I like my shoes loose and sloppy. If I wanted snug, I would have bought a pair of cheap sneakers a size too small. You don't get more snug than that, and you'll save about $130.

Still they jog by—all sizes, shapes and colours. From my hammock I watch an endless procession. It's like a fashion show—every conceivable outfit is worn by these people. Some are conservative, some are really wild. There is a guy going by right now who is wearing blue jeans and a heavy, black leather jacket. Right behind him is another with a policeman's uniform on. Surely it is too hot for outfits like those. Hold it! Maybe they aren't joggers; the guy in the policeman's outfit is putting handcuffs on the guy in the black leather jacket. Scrub those two! But there are plenty more behind them. The funny part is most of them look to be in great shape. About 90 per cent of them need jogging like a moose needs a hat rack. None of them seem to have a clue that jogging is a very dangerous sport.

Take the young lady down the street, for example. She's just about perfect. A beautiful face, lovely hair, a perfect shape—in fact, everything about her is perfect. Well, maybe not everything. Her eyes can't be too good or she would have seen the open manhole. Under the circumstances, perhaps we had better call it a 'personhole' or 'peoplehole'—although she is the only lady I ever saw go down one.

This, serious as it was, was nothing compared to what happened to Arthur—poor Arthur. Arthur always ended the last hundred yards of his daily jog with a very fast run. We will probably never know how fast he was going when he hit the truck that was unloading sixteen cubic yards of very fast drying cement. Fortunately, it was not a total loss. The truck driver and his helper had the presence of mind to stand him on his feet before the stuff set, and someone else folded Arthur's arms around a large plastic bowl—which they later filled with water.

Arthur is now a birdbath on South Park Street. If you wave to him as you go by, I'm sure you will understand why he does not wave back.

If these people had been lying in a hammock sipping a glass of cold beer, they would both be, if not in perfect shape, at least still breathing today. A little quiet dissipation never hurt anyone.

As I write this, two large robins have landed on our lawn. They are hopping over to where my wife has left some sunflower seeds. The way they are hopping makes them look like they are jogging and this proves conclusively what I have been saying all along: Jogging is for the birds.

Chapter 21
Hear the Salvia Shriek?

Several years ago I read an article in a leading science magazine that stated trees, flowers and other growing things had feelings. At first I read this with a feeling of disbelief—I felt they were putting me on but then they offered proof that was very convincing. It seems they somehow hooked a galvanometer to various plants; and, by measuring fluctuations in the electrical field, they proved that plants respond to stimuli. Suddenly it was believable.

After all, the impulses from the human brain are electrical and it is possible to measure them and determine their response to stress or other incitement, so why not flowers and trees. The article went on to state that trees can communicate with each other. They cited an example of one tree being infested by a certain type of bug and passing this information on to neighbouring trees, which then produced a chemical that made them unattractive to that particular bug. This proved to me that growing things think, react and communicate. Trees are lucky—I wish I could produce a chemical that would make me unattractive to some of the things that bug me.

The part that disturbed me was when they said that trees, flowers and growing things actually scream when they are cut or abused! When I thought of all the ragweed and dandelions I had uprooted over the years, I felt terrible! I'm really a very gentle soul and I would never knowingly inflict pain.

I don't get a chance any more. My wife won't even let me weed since I cleaned out that bed of salvia I thought was crabgrass. The only thing I'm allowed to look after is the rhubarb behind the garage. This is because I know the secret of truly great rhubarb. I was taught by my father. Every time I wash my feet, I pour the used water on the rhubarb patch. By midsummer any one leaf provides shade for four adults or six children. The stalks are well over seven feet tall and have to be cut with a chain saw. Is that rhubarb or what? Everyone says it is delicious, the best they've ever tasted. Personally, I've never tried it, and I don't intend to.

Each year we have a very extensive garden. Almost every square inch of the property is a blaze of glory during the growing season. But I am only allowed to do the digging and shovelling, add the peat moss and the manure and mix the whole thing up; I'm not allowed to do any of the planting. That's from the time I planted the gladioli bulbs upside down; nothing came up. According to my wife you probably would have had to dig down three feet to see the flowers.

Another thing the article said was you should talk to your plants; they respond positively to the calm tones of the human voice. I have trouble with this. I never know what to say. In the first place, I don't know whether they are boy petunias or girl petunias. I hate to bring sex into this but the gender determines the type of language I might use. To play it safe, I usually confine myself to some inane remarks like, "Hi, there, how's it goin'?" or "Hey, you're lookin' good!" Sometimes I'll ask a direct question like, "Need some water?" or "How about a shot of sheep manure?" I always feel very self-conscious and the plants pay no attention to me—nothing else does, why should they?

My wife has no problem. She speaks to them, they

understand and they respond. This had me mystified until one day I overheard the conversation she was having with a newly planted bed of impatiens. Smiling sweetly she said, "All right, you cruddy plants, listen up. This is Tuesday. We have company coming Sunday afternoon, and I want this place a mass of dazzling colour. Any plants that are not in full bloom by noon Sunday are going to be ripped up by the roots and slammed down into the compost heap."

If you could have hooked up a galvanometer to them at that point, the stress reading would probably have run right off the scale. Well, by Sunday everything looked gorgeous. In fact, a local old-timer looked at our garden on his way by and said, "This is prettier than the Hanging Gardens of Babylon or the Garden of Eden."

He should know—he saw them both when he was a young man. And this proves that when you are talking to plants, a little fear and intimidation is more effective than a thousand kind words.

Chapter 22
You've Come a Long Way, Lady

In the beginning, after God created the heavens and the earth, He gazed at the wonders He had wrought and felt a little sad. There were rainbows to see, flowers to smell, birds to hear but no one to appreciate the beauty He had created. And so it came to pass, as an afterthought, God created man.

This was not one of his better efforts. I attribute this to exhaustion. After all, creating man after you have just finished the earth and the firmament (in less than a week, I might add) would be like slapping together a cheap garden shed after you've finished building the Taj Mahal. It's understandable that things might get a little sloppy.

Right from the start He had trouble with Adam, for Adam was a whiner. Even living in the Garden of Eden he had complaints. He had no one to blame when he made a mistake. It takes two to tango. He couldn't travel anywhere because he had no one to read the map. He hated housework! There was no one to admire his manly virtues and his superior intellect.

So God appeared to Adam and said, "Boy, do I have the girl for you!" and following the first successful rib transplant, God created Eve. There are many people, including me, who feel this produced a finer product than the first hurried effort with the lump of clay.

But right from this very beginning women were treated as second-class citizens. If you read the Gospel according to Saint Matthew, you will notice that all the begettings were male. Abraham begat Isaac; and Isaac begat Jacob; and Jacob begat Judas and his brethren. (You will note there is no mention of 'sisterthren'), and this went on for fourteen generations, ending with David begetting Solomon of her that had been the wife of Urias, which shows there was a certain amount of hanky-panky even then. Then for fourteen more generations, starting with Solomon begetting Roboam and ending with Josias begetting Jechonias, there is no mention of women being begot. And then another fourteen generations go by, ending with Jacob begat Joseph, the husband of Mary. Finally a woman is mentioned by name.

I think they only did it then because she was a saint. But there must have been a lot more women than Mary. What did all these men begat with—chopped liver? To begat you have to have a begettee and a begetter or nothing can begot. I believe the ladies weren't mentioned because of male dominance. I can almost hear Adam screaming, "Waddaya mean, you need a new fig leaf; you've a closet full of fig leaves, what's wrong with them?" Or, generations later, a caveman yelling at his cave-spouse, "If you'd shut up for a few minutes I would've got that sabre-toothed tiger and we'd have plenty to eat. I can't concentrate when you're yakking at me!" (All she was trying to tell him was he should use the pointed end of the spear.)

And so it has been for thousands of years. Women have been put down and denied equality. I have always made it a point to assure every woman I've ever met that I am an exception. I consider them to be equal to me. For some reason, this does not fill them with joy.

It is only in the last hundred years that they have taken giant steps towards their goal. In 1892, during an all-comers boxing exhibition in Arkansas, a lady by the name of Hessie Donahue climbed into the ring with world-heavyweight champion John L. Sullivan and knocked him senseless. So much for superior male strength. From 1885 to 1901, Annie Oakley shot cigarettes out of her husband's mouth every day of the week in Buffalo Bill's Wild West Show. They say he was a very mild-mannered man who wouldn't dream of talking back and was only too happy to quit smoking.

You've come a long way, lady. From not having the vote, you now have men voting for you. We've had a woman prime minister for Great Britain, India and Canada. Women are training for combat roles in the military and we had a woman as Minister of Defence. You are in every field—doctors, lawyers, social workers, accountants, truck drivers, engineers, and everything else you can name. You are getting closer every day and I wish you well.

Chapter 23
You Can't Trust Those Bureaucrats!

Several months ago I had a phone call from the Department of Veterans Affairs telling me I qualified for the Veterans Independence Program (V.I.P.). They said I would be eligible for new glasses, hearing aids, wheelchair or any other health aid I might need, free of any charge. Furthermore, they would pay the expense of lawn mowing, snow shovelling and leaf raking (my wife was very happy to hear about those three) again without cost to me. Now, to tell you the truth this sounded like 'pie in the sky' to me and I greeted this with a certain amount of skepticism; after all, I have had some less than marvellous encounters with bureaucrats over my many years. To tell you the absolute truth, and I know this will shock you, the faith I have in bureaucrats ranks far below the faith I have in the veracity of the stories in *National Enquirer.*

Nevertheless, I did need new glasses. To be absolutely certain of their intentions, I called the department and said, "As I understand it, since I qualify under your Veterans Independence Program, I am entitled to buy new glasses and your department will pay the entire cost, is that true?" The man said, "Yes, sir, you go get your new glasses and we will pay for them, they won't cost you one cent."

Well, it couldn't be plainer than that, so the next day I went shopping for new glasses. I bought forty-eight wine glasses, twenty-four large beer glasses, twenty-four cocktail glasses and six dozen tumblers. I felt good about this because all my old glasses were chipped and scratched, especially the beer glasses—they had received a lot of hard usage.

When they got the bill you should have heard the squawk. I told you, didn't I? You can't trust those people. They reneged on their promise and now I have to pay for them myself. So much for their stupid V.I.P. program! So much for bureaucratic promises!

Upsetting as that was, the attitude of the clerk in the store where I bought the glasses perturbed me even more. It was a prestige establishment; one of those places where you pay more for the name than you do for the product. But in places like that you run into some clerks who have a superiority complex; they look down their nose at mere peasants. Their rate of pay, in dollars, is directly proportional to the length of their nose in centimetres. At 9.4 cm, the man who waited on me was the highest paid person in the store. He must have taken his sales training at Tiffany's on Fifth Avenue because when I picked out some wine glasses I liked and asked the price, he said, "Sir, if you have to ask the price, you can't afford them; those particular glasses are forty-five dollars each." He's right, I can't afford them, but I said, "Buddy, I'm a big tipper and I have to know the price so I can calculate the tip."

That did it. His attitude changed instantly from arrogant to obsequious. I could see him calculating 20 per cent of forty-eight glasses at $45 each, and for the rest of the buying spree the service was excellent. Before I finished my conscience bothered me. I am a very patriotic type person. Every morning while I am shaving, I stand at attention and sing the national anthem, with tears in my eyes. A loyal, conscientious citizen like me would be the very last person in the world to even think of playing havoc with the governments deficit, so I bought the $28.50 beer glasses instead of the $30 ones. Believe me, saving the government $36 gives us patriots a really warm feeling.

When I finished I wrote on a cheque form, sealed it in an envelope and gave it to the clerk, "This is for you, in appreciation of your splendid service." He beamed, put it in his pocket and carried all the boxes to the car. Then he came back and carried me to the car. I got out of there fast.

Now I've got a problem. I can't pay for the glasses, the government won't pay for them, I can't return them for a refund because by now he's opened the envelope and found the cheque form on which I wrote, "HERE'S YOUR TIP, PAL: DON'T PLAY WITH MATCHES."

If any of you need new glasses, please get in touch—I'm sure we can make a deal. Meanwhile, I'm checking this free hearing aid thing. Surely a new stereo system would qualify as a hearing aid.

Chapter 24
The New Account

To tell you the absolute truth, I have never really trusted banks. I admire them, I must admit that. How could you not admire an outfit that consistently posted monstrous great profits every year during a major recession? Each year as more and more businesses went bankrupt and thousands were unemployed, bank profits steadily climbed to astronomical heights. But trust them? No way. So whenever I have a little extra cash, which is seldom, I just put it in a bowl or something and hide it in my closet. But recently a friend of mine, whose financial shrewdness I have always admired, told me that I was a fool to keep my life's savings at home. He explained that by keeping it in the house I took the risk of losing it, having it stolen or destroyed by fire. This made sense. Besides, he explained, if I put it in the bank I would earn interest on it and this would add to my yearly income. Now if there is anyone in this whole world who needs to add to their yearly income, it's me. Then, shortly after I was talking to him, I won the money on that lottery ticket and I decided maybe it was time that I followed his advice.

When I told the lady at the bank that I wanted to open an account and put all my money where it was safe, she seemed ever so happy. She gave me a wonderful, warm smile and asked me to wait while she got a form. In a few minutes she returned with a large, printed page that she said was a questionnaire for new depositors. Now if there is anything I like less than banks, it's answering a whole lot of questions; I'm a very private sort of person. But she seemed so friendly and sincere I just didn't have the heart to get her upset, and I must admit that in the beginning it did not seem too bad. It asked me to print my name, address and phone number. This seemed very logical. They have to know whose money it is and where they can get in touch with me. They probably need the phone number so they can call me every few days to let me know that my money is still safe and they are taking good care of it.

But then the questions started to get personal. They wanted to know my social insurance number and what other banks I had money in and what was the source of this capital. They wanted to know who was my next of kin, where I worked and how much I made, and if I owned my own home and my marital status; at this point I started to get very upset. Frankly, I felt that none of this was any of their business.

If I completed this form they would know everything about me and I would know nothing about them. This did not make sense. Would you hand over your life savings and your lottery winnings to perfect strangers? Of course you wouldn't. Well neither would I. After all, I'm trusting them to look after my money. I would only fill out that form if they were going to entrust me with theirs.

So I went back home and made up a questionnaire for them—I have to know something about these people before I hand over all my cash. I went back the next day and gave the lady my questionnaire and asked her to call me when she had it completed. That was three months ago; I haven't heard from them since.

Here is the questionnaire:

1. Is the bank manager happily married or is there some truth to the rumour that he is fooling around with a teller?

2. Does the manager or the assistant manager display more than an average interest in horse racing, bingo, lottery

tickets, dice, roulette or stud poker?

3. Has there been any talk of a Las Vegas vacation by any of the personnel who know the combination to the vault?

4. Why do you chain down a cheap pen that doesn't work?

5. Are any of the bank officers:

a. Receiving travel brochures that describe expensive, exotic trips to foreign countries?

b. Driving luxury cars that are obviously beyond their income?

6. Why does your accountant have that cat-ate-the-canary smile? Has he just put something over on somebody? If so, was that somebody a depositor at this bank?

7. Have any of the tellers been nipping at the cooking sherry during coffee break?

8. Why do 90 per cent of the tellers head for the back room when the bank gets full of customers? What's going on back there? Does it involve fooling around? Or the cooking sherry? Or a combination thereof?

9. Are there plans to lend another zillion dollars to Mexico or any third world countries; if so, will my money be part of it?

10. Is anyone in this bank related in any way, no matter how remotely, to Willie Sutton, John Dillinger or 'Bugs' Moran?

The answers to these questions are important to me. Based on this information, I will make my decision. If I am not happy with some of their answers, I will take my life savings ($186.35) plus the $66 I won for having four of the numbers in the lottery, to another financial institution.

On second thought, maybe I should just take my wife and a few friends to dinner at a high class restaurant and blow the whole bit on a really nice dinner and a few drinks—then I won't have to worry about it.

Chapter 25
Inspirational Messages

*Two men gazed from behind prison bars. One
looked down and saw the mud. The other looked
up and saw the stars.*

Anonymous

This inspirational message, as you can see, was written by
an ancient Greek philosopher named Anonymous. I know
for sure he is ancient because I have been reading his stuff
since I was a kid, and I'm getting fairly ancient myself. I'm
also pretty sure he is Greek—any name ending in 'ous' has
got to be Greek. (There is a Mr. Papodopolous who runs a
Greek restaurant near here.)

What I am not too sure about is that he is a he. I have
never seen his first name written anywhere, so there is a
possibility that he is a she. If his full name is Annie
Anonymous, then he would have to be a Miss, Mrs., or Ms.

The reason this thought occurs to me is the fact that
much of what he/she/whomever says happens to sound
like some of the stuff my wife says from time to time.
When I blew a bundle on the big birthday bash last year,
she hit me with, "A fool and his money are some party."

If that doesn't sound like Anonymous, what does?

Regardless of gender, Anonymous wrote some pretty
good stuff, and I have found inspirational guidance for my
own life from his little gems of philosophy. Take the one at
the beginning of this column for example. I always look up
and see the stars. Suppose we are in the midst of a howling

blizzard for the fourth day in a row, and my neighbour is shovelling snow from his driveway for the tenth time; I love to spread the philosophy of good cheer by yelling, "Look at the bright side—there are no mosquitoes or black flies." It is generally wiser to yell this from a distance—those steel snow shovels can really smart.

Another gem of guidance that has been an influence on my behavioral pattern is:

> There is so much good
> in the worst of us
> and so much bad
> in the best of us,
> that it ill behooves
> any of us to criticize
> the rest of us.
>   Anonymous

This allows me to forgive my wife for things like the "fool and his money" routine or the "sauce for the goose is sauce for the gander" bit.

One person who was greatly influenced by an inspirational message was the captain of a British battleship during World War II. Every morning this man would go to his desk, remove a well-worn black book, open it to a book-marked page and slowly, carefully, read the message inscribed. He would close the book, gaze upward in silent meditation for a few moments and then reverently return the book to the drawer. Even in the midst of battle, with enemy shells and bombs exploding all around and torpedoes zipping by, the captain would go to the drawer and again read those precious words. Returning to his position of command he would quietly and gently say, "Helmsman, come hard-a-port, please." And sure enough, that was the one right manoeuvre to save the ship from destruction. Bombs would land and the wake of torpedoes would churn through where the ship would have been except for this divinely inspired move.

The crew held him in esteem that bordered on idolatry, and his crew was the envy of every other ship in the British Navy, for he ran a 'safe ship.' Everyone knew that his brilliant seamanship would save them from enemy action.

Just before the end of the war the captain died. He was not killed by enemy action, he just quietly passed away in his sleep. His magnificent heart stopped beating. There was not a dry eye on the ship the day they committed his body to the waters of the ocean he knew and loved so well.

That night, after the service, they reverently opened the drawer to at last reveal the secret, inspirational message that had made this man the master seaman he had proven to be. The message was:

> If you are standing in the middle of the ship (called midship) and are looking toward the sharp end (called the bow) then all that stuff over on your left is called port and the stuff on the other side (your right) is called starboard. Have a really nice day.
>
> P.S. The guy steering the thing is called the Helmsman.

Chapter 26
Blessed Are the Clowns

Every now and then I suffer from a pinched nerve in my neck. This, although not life-threatening, can be annoying and painful; to alleviate the pain, I have to wear a cervical collar. Now, this looks much worse than it actually is. The collar is heavily padded and has a notch to fit under your chin and velcro fasteners to adjust it to your neck size. The purpose is to support the weight of your head and relieve the pressure on the pinched nerve. It does just that and is quite comfortable to wear. But it looks terrible.

Friends who saw you yesterday, without the collar and obviously the picture of buoyant good health, now see a pathetic invalid whose head is anchored rigidly by a monstrous great contraption. They figure you have been in at least a five-car pile-up or have fallen off the observation platform at the Empire State Building. With a look of shock and in a voice tinged with sympathy and concern they exclaim, "Good Lord, what in the name of Heaven happened to you?" Now is the time to use your 'cervical collar' routine.

With a puzzled frown and a timid voice you say, "I'm not quite sure, it all happened so fast. I remember I was talking with my wife, well actually we weren't talking, we were arguing and she said something to me and I said something to her and then she said something to me and the last thing I remember was sneering and saying, 'Oh, yeah! You and how many helpers, honey?' When I came to, the emergency room people were fitting this thing on my neck."

A simple little comic routine, such as this, can bring laughter to many people, and we all need far more laughter in our lives. It is a pity that the Beatitudes in the Sermon on the Mount giving praise to the "meek," the "peacekeepers" and the "pure in heart" do not give equal praise to the clowns. There should be one that says, "Blessed are the clowns for they bring joy to the heart." Laughter is not only beneficial to the heart, it also causes the brain to release endorphin, a natural pain killer as effective as morphine, and if laughter should become addictive—so much the better. Only now is medical science realizing the full benefit of laughter as the best medicine.

I personally lack the courage to be a true clown. I don't mind the 'cervical collar' bit, but you would never get me to do the 'eye doctor' routine. My friend, Bob, does this one every time he has to go for an eye exam. The medical clinic has about fifteen doctors; three or four are general practitioners, the rest are specialists, including an ophthalmologist. Bob borrows a pair of glasses that look like the bottoms of coke bottles. With these on he slowly and hesitantly enters the common waiting room where perhaps twenty patients are sitting. Doubled over and squinting furiously, he bumps into the first empty chair and in his best W. C. Fields voice snarls, "Why don't you go sit down, kid, before you get hurt!" He then bumps into the receptionist's desk, mutters, "Sorry sir," and looks wildly around the room. About six feet away is a coat rack holding a raincoat and a hat. With renewed confidence, Bob marches up to within a few feet of the raincoat and screams, "Hi! I got an appointment for 3:30—are you the eye doctor?"

By now everyone in the room is laughing. The endorphin is flowing and hearts are full of joy. People, who a few moments ago were studiously ignoring each other, avoiding eye contact and trying to get interested in a two-

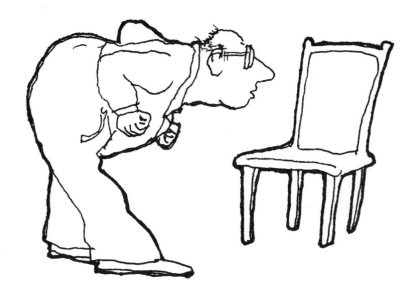

year-old magazine, are now smiling and talking. Laughter has worked its magic.

One routine I never dared was the time my wife had to go to the hospital by ambulance. She had suffered a fall and the doctor wanted X-rays to ascertain damage. As they were putting the stretcher in the ambulance, I had an overwhelming desire to step out on the porch with my apron and chef's hat on and wave a large mixing spoon at her and scream, "Next time you'll eat what I bloody well cook!" But my fear of personal injury deterred me. That and the fact she probably would have yelled back, "That's why they're taking me to the hospital—I ate what you bloody well cooked!" I hate being one-upped.

Chapter 27
The Millionaire

One of the major problems that I have encountered in life is that my out-go has always exceeded my in-come. I have never had what I consider to be enough money to live in the manner to which I would like to become accustomed. I never did, I don't now and I probably never will. This problem was precipitated by my tendency to spend money I don't have, buying things I don't need, to impress people I don't like. This is not a dilemma that is unique; I'm sure that a great many people in this world have a similar problem. So, when I meet a person who makes more in interest on their investments per week than I make in a year's work, I regard them with a fascination that approaches awe. What is it about these people that makes them worth millions of dollars? How did they do it? What secret lies behind the acquisition of such wealth?

When I was thirty years of age I found out the secret; and now, free of any charge or stipulation, I will pass it on to you. That year began as a very difficult time for me. I had just started my own business and my cash flow wasn't flowing. I had left the security of a steady salary and was desperately trying to build up a clientele; it was a slow process. My wife and I had bought a new home that was covered with a wall-to-wall mortgage being paid by back-to-the-wall financing. It did have a beautiful view—on a clear day you could see all the expenses hanging over my head. I could not get any assistance from the bank, the manager and I had only a nodding acquaintance—I didn't do nodding for him and he certainly didn't do nodding for me.

To say that times were financially tight is indubitably the understatement of that or any other year. During this personal recession, I met Charles who became a friend as well as a very good customer. Charles was a millionaire but it was not possible to discern this by his appearance. He didn't look different from other people. The only thing that seemed to set him apart was that everyone called him Charles. He was never Charlie or Chuck. Charlies and Chucks don't have that kind of money. He was Charles with a big capital "C" and you drew his name out so that it had a resonance that set it apart from ordinary non-millionaire-type Charleses.

In the beginning of our friendship I could not for the life of me figure out how he had earned a fortune. He was not very smart, at least about the ordinary things of life; if you handed him any sharp tool he grabbed it by the wrong end and cut himself. He wasn't handy, he couldn't build anything, he couldn't fix anything. The more I saw of him, the more baffled I became. But then one day I had the opportunity to question him in depth about his money and how he made it—and the secret was revealed.

It came about one day when Charles invited me to be his guest for lunch at the hotel. Since I was getting just a wee bit bored with peanut butter sandwiches, I accepted. When we arrived at the hotel we were seated, with great deference, at the best table, and the waiters, Maitre d' and the hotel manager hovered at a respectful distance ready to instantly gratify his every whim. Charles asked me what I would like to have for lunch and I told him that I never had a big lunch, just usually a hamburger or some fish and chips. He leaned over and whispered, "The chef in this hotel spent fourteen years training in the finest restaurants of Paris, then another five years in Rome. He is probably one of the top three master chefs in North America. If you order hamburger or fish and chips, you will inflict a mortal wound to his ego from which he will never recover. Besides, there are no wines that go with fish and chips. May I suggest that you have the lobster thermidor, followed by chocolate mousse and a steaming hot cup of Irish coffee, and please, leave the wine selection to me."

He is way over my head, I'm definitely a fish and chips type of person, and Irish coffee sounds awful; who could possibly enjoy green coffee. But I liked the word lobster and I liked the word chocolate and I trusted Charles so I simply said, "Sounds great."

While I was enjoying the lobster thermidor—and believe me, it was delicious—I noticed that Charles was having a small plate of cheese and crackers with a large glass of milk.

"Aren't you having the lobster," I asked. "It's great."

"I can't," he said, "stomach ulcers and high blood pressure."

A little later on I had a glance at the bill; and, judging by the price, they must have been gourmet crackers, or maybe the milk wasn't regular milk, it could have been goat's milk flown in from Tibet, fresh that morning, especially for him. The bill was slightly higher than the amount my wife and I spent on a month's groceries.

After lunch, while I am finishing my Irish coffee (and a few mugs of this stuff could ease a lot of pain), I asked him point-blank, "Charles, I know you are a millionaire, and this is just idle curiosity on my part—you don't have to tell me if you don't want to—just how much money are you worth?"

He said, "No, I don't mind answering; according to my accountants, last year I was worth forty-seven million dollars." I felt like someone had belted me in the stomach with a sledge hammer. I almost lost my lobster thermidor, three glasses of wine, chocolate mousse and two mugs of Irish coffee. He's saying this to a man who is going to have to borrow enough from a finance company to pay off some of the bank loan so he can go on an overdraft. It is several minutes before I can speak.

"Forty-seven million! Forty-seven million! How in the name of all that's holy does anyone get that kind of money?"

"Well, it's really very simple." I broke in with, "Simple ... simple! I'm kind of simple and I don't have forty-seven bucks."

He said, "Look, there are all kinds of ways of making money. I know one guy, a friend of mine, that made over a million in the last few years just by playing poker; are you any good at poker?"

My mind flashed back to my first few days in the Air Force during the War. A sergeant came up to me one night and said, "How much money you got, kid?"

I said, "I have twenty-eight dollars, sir."

"Don't call me sir, son, I'm not a commissioned officer, just call me your majesty or your highness. Do you know how to play poker?"

I said, "No sir, ah, your majesty."

"Okay, kid, come over here and I'll give you your first lesson." Ten minutes later I had my first lesson and he had my twenty-eight dollars.

I snapped back to the present. "I'm afraid that I'm no good at poker, Charles."

"Well don't worry about it," he said. "That's only one way out of thousands. You have to think of something that's needed by the public and then supply that need. I was just thinking of something the other day, there is someone I know who is in the hospital for a heart transplant, fellow by the name of O'Reilly. Now, I went to one of the card shops looking for a card to send him, and every card in the store had all kinds of mushy stuff on it about 'getting well soon,' 'wishing you well,' 'hope to see you home real soon,' and that kind of garbage."

I said, "Well, yeah, what's wrong with that?"

"What's wrong with it is I don't like O'Reilly. In fact I hate O'Reilly, and it seems to me there must be thousands of people in hospital, or sick, that other people dislike. So there should be a fortune for the person who comes up with a line of 'stay sick' cards."

"I don't understand," I said. This guy was going too fast for me. "How would that work?"

"Easy," Charles said. "On the cover you could have a cartoon of someone who is sick as a dog and right below that, in large letters it would say 'STAY SICK, SUCKER,' and then when you open it up, inside would be a cute little verse, maybe something like:

Roses are red
Violets are blue
I hope when you get out
You come down with the flu.

And while you're at it there is probably a pretty good market for 'Bah! Humbug' cards for those of us that are not too fussy about Christmas."

My head is swimming and I'm making notes as fast as I can.

"Is that how you made your money, Charles?"

"Oh, no." he said. "I'm no good at anything like that—I made my money by investing. You buy something, hold on to it for a little while and then sell it. Then you invest that money plus the profit into stocks and bonds and then take that profit and reinvest it and it just sort of snowballs into big money."

"Gee," I said, "it sounds easy enough; is it?"

"No, it certainly is not easy. You have to use every ounce of your energy and give it your total concentration.

You have to work at it to the exclusion of everything else in life. You can't have hobbies, your social life suffers, every moment of your life is focused on the acquisition of money. It's money, money, money, every minute of the day."

"And is that how you made forty-seven million dollars?" I asked reverently.

"Yes it is," he said. "That's the secret; and, of course, another thing that helped me quite a bit was when my father died last year—he left me sixty-five million dollars."

Well, there it was—I had the answer. It's not my fault that I'm not a millionaire, it's my father's. He didn't leave me sixty-five million dollars; in fact, all he left me was a pocket watch that doesn't work and a model schooner in a whisky bottle that looks like whoever built it drank the whisky moments before they started building the schooner. Actually, he didn't give me the schooner, he sold it to me for eight dollars. But he did bequeath me his Irish wit and his irreverent sense of humour; that's worth a fortune to me. And, look on the bright side, I don't have to eat those gourmet crackers and cheese, and drink that yucky imported goat's milk.

Chapter 28
Goodness Snakes Alive!

One of the most effective ways to overcome the fear of something is to learn everything you can about the subject. It's called "know the enemy." Most of the time this works. If you really understand the thing you fear, you probably will no longer fear it. Now that I've convinced you of that, I have to tell you it may not be true. Many people suffer from more than one phobia. If you happen to suffer from "agoraphobia," the fear of open spaces, and simultaneously from "claustrophobia," the fear of enclosed spaces, you are between a rock and a hard place. You can't go out and you can't stay in. And, if you suffer from "eremophobia," fear of being alone, and "ochlophobia," the fear of other people, then you don't have anyone to go out or stay in with! But that's your problem—I have enough phobias of my own.

Ever since I was a kid, I've had a horrible fear of insects, spiders and other creepy, crawly things— "arachniphobia." I also go into a screaming tizzy over crocodiles and alligators—"batrachophobia"; but, by far, the fear that reduces me to a quivering, cowering, craven chicken is my fear of snakes—"ophidiophobia."

The fact that I was born and lived in an area completely free of poisonous snakes, spiders, crocodiles and other such creatures didn't influence me one bit. I've never been the type of person to let a few facts deter me from being completely unreasonable.

And then, during World War II, a wonderful thing

happened! The Royal Air Force sent me to Sierra Leone, West Africa! How lucky can you get! For a year and a half I was not only surrounded by all the slithering creatures that petrify an ophidiophobic but I was able to quickly develop two new phobias: the fear of jungles and the fear of swamps; there isn't even Latin names for those yet. No one ever had a better opportunity to "know the enemy." In addition to huge tarantulas, we had scorpions, bush spiders, centipedes and a host of other creepy, crawly things. That was just on the ground. In the water we had crocodiles, snakes, leeches and other slithering, slimy things. Take your pick. Even the air wasn't safe. It was loaded with bugs, beetles, killer bees, tsetse flies, anopheles mosquitoes and aedes aegyptic mosquitoes; the last three mentioned killed more people with yellow fever, malaria and sleeping sickness than all the wars since time began.

But, above all, we had snakes. We had some of the most delightful snakes ever created. There was the "boomslang" a rear-fanged, tree-dwelling snake about six feet long that was completely harmless according to Mr. Karl P. Schmidt, and he should know. He was considered to be the world's leading authority on snakes. In fact, even as he lay dying after being bitten by one, he didn't believe it, he kept muttering, "It musta bin somethin' I et!"

In addition to the boomslang, we also had the puff adder, gaboon viper, the spitting cobra, pit viper, green mamba and the black mamba. The green mamba is only half as long as the ten-foot black mamba, but I understand that he's just as deadly as the 'ripe' one. Since, in addition to the boomslang, both mambas are tree climbers, I decided to forgo my Tarzan routine of swinging through the jungle on vines. With my eyesight, I could be swinging from mamba to boomslang. I learned a great deal about snakes in the year and a half I was in Africa. The most important thing—snakes are not dangerous. They will only strike if they feel threatened and cannot escape. This means that there are a lot of paranoid snakes out there, because forty thousand people die each year from snake bite. It would take all the sharks in the world over one hundred years to kill that many people, not that I'm overly thrilled with sharks, either.

The next thing—all snakes are deaf. There goes the old 'snake charmer' myth. When the snake rears up in the basket and weaves to and fro, he's not listening to the flute. He doesn't care if you are playing Brahms' Lullaby, "Jailhouse Rock" or the Third Movement from Ex-Lax; he simply sees the charmer as a menace and assumes a position to strike. The charmer, far from being stupid, knows he cannot come closer without being struck, so it's a standoff; neither can move until the other has gone.

The black mamba is the fastest snake in the world; it can travel between seven and ten miles per hour—about as fast as most people can run. The moment I found this out I immediately convulsed into great gales of laughter and completely lost my fear of snakes. When I see any snake, I'm loping along at a little over a hundred and twenty miles an hour—in the opposite direction. The fool thing is not even in the same race.

Chapter 29
Hi Jack!

Just about a year ago I was at the international airport and I saw Jack, a friend of mine, at the other end of the concourse. I knew I couldn't catch up to him, so I yelled "Hi Jack!" I didn't get his attention but I did get the attention of five members of the anti-terrorist squad, three security guards, the top brass of the international airport and a humongous, great guard dog. Within ten seconds I was pinned face down on the floor by the security people while the anti-terrorist types frisked me for bombs or weapons, and the guard dog licked my face. It seems that 'hijack' is not something you should yell at an international airport, not even when it is two separate words.

While I was lying there, with my nose flattened on the floor and my hands handcuffed in a painful position behind my back, I said to myself, "My goodness, how the meaning of words has changed since I was young. What used to be a friendly salutation has now become an intimidating expletive." There were several hours of questions about political affiliations and possible membership in various terrorist groups. I managed to convince them that the only group I had ever belonged to was the Rinkydinks. This was a mildly dangerous group of ten-year-olds whose only notable crime was knocking the hat off the local bank manager with a snowball one Easter Sunday morning. They eventually conceded that the Rinkydinks were not really a massive threat to national security and did not warrant the full attention of the anti-terrorist people, F.B.I., Interpol, and whomever. I was released.

On my way home I was listening to rock music on the car radio and I said, "There's another thing that has changed meaning." When I was young, 'hard rock' was something immovable that you found halfway down a post-hole you were trying to dig. For 'soft rock,' you put a feather pillow on granny's rocking chair. We had "pot" but you didn't smoke it—you cooked stuff in it. People didn't come out of closets; overcoats, galoshes, scarves and hats did. We had 'grass' and 'coke,' but you didn't smoke it and sniff it; you mowed it and drank it, in that order.

A few years ago I took some computer courses. In the back of one textbook there was a glossary of computer words and their meaning. There were hundreds of words; many of them were words I used to know as something else. A 'HARD DRIVE' was from here to anywhere with the narrow, winding, and unbelievably rough dirt and gravel roads we had then. 'BACK UP' was something you did, in your 1933 Plymouth, if you forgot to stop for a beautiful brunette, a stunning blonde or a ravishing redhead. If you had a really big mouth, you could take a 'MEGABYTE' out of an 'APPLE,' especially if it was a 'MACINTOSH.' We didn't have 'FLOPPY DISKS' but if we had, my mother would have starched them. 'BOOTING' was something violent that kids got if they aggravated an adult, and 'DEFAULT' was something that was always 'de other guys.'

Dot Matrix lived just down the street from my house. I always called her Mrs. Matrix because she was much older than I was, and I used to run errands for her. A very nice lady; I remember her well.

We also had 'CHARACTERS' but they weren't letters, numbers and symbols. One lived next door to Mrs. Matrix; he was an old guy who always wore spats over his sneakers, had a big turkey feather in his bowler hat and smacked every second lamppost with his umbrella. I tried not to 'ENTER' a conversation with him.

A 'HARD COPY' was trying to read the smart kid's 'WORDPERFECT' answers off his exam paper from three desks away. If he was so smart, why didn't he write larger? The only 'BELLS AND WHISTLES' were on trains, and a 'MOUSE' was a cute, little furry creature that I tried to protect from the traps my Dad set. The only time I liked to see a 'NETWORK' was when I was catching butterflies for my collection.

No wonder I'm confused most of the time! When someone says something to me now, I have to figure out which meaning to give the words—B.C. (before computers) or A.D. (after the Depression).

Chapter 30
Oh! Hear Dem Chimes

About a year ago it suddenly dawned on me that maybe everyone was not mumbling after all; maybe there was something wrong with my hearing. To tell you the truth, to this point I had never found it an insurmountable problem because almost everywhere I went, my wife was with me and to really mess up a metaphor, 'She has ears like a hawk.' When we were with a group of people and someone would mumble at me, I had merely to turn to her, raise an eyebrow, and she would translate what they said into intelligible words.

She also has endless patience; she doesn't mind repeating things six or seven times at progressively increasing volume. If all else fails, my wife is a genius at charades. Many a time, at a noisy party, she would jump up and act out what someone was trying to tell me. This created a sense of fun and soon everyone in the room was on their feet acting out what they were talking about; and this, of course, eliminated the necessity of hearing them; I could see what they were saying—there is nothing wrong with my eyes.

The thing that finally persuaded me to get a hearing test occurred one night when my wife was out shopping. I had finally managed to find a copy of a book at the library that I had been looking forward to reading entitled, *A Beginners Guide to Frontal Lobotomies Using Simple Garden Tools*. I love reading, especially educational stuff. So when she came home, in the driving rain, I was stretched out in my chair in the living room engrossed in the wonderful world of science. Obviously she had misplaced her key so she rang the front door chimes.

Now, as it happens, those chimes are on the same frequency as my tinnitus and they get lost among the whistle, whine and warble that I hear all the time. Fortunately, about a half-hour later I ran out of goodies and had to go to the kitchen to replenish my supply. As I went through the hall I saw her standing in the rain, leaning on the doorbell. She looked a little peeved. I thought about it for a moment or two and then decided to open the door. She was a little peeved, "Do you realize I've been standing here in the rain, ringing the bell, for the last half-hour; didn't you hear the chime?"

I very reasonably said, "Of course I hear the chimes, I've been hearing chimes for the last fifty years, ever since I fired that stupid machine gun back in '43, I just didn't realize it was your chime."

Well, that was the turning point, it was a choice between getting a hearing aid or putting up with a soggy, peeved wife; and, as most husbands will tell you, that's not really a choice. I made an appointment to be tested for a hearing aid.

It got off to a bad start from the very first sentence. When I walked into the office the receptionist said, "Good morning, isn't this a lovely day?" I said, "I didn't bring enough money with me to pay, you'll have to bill me." Then she said, "Are you Mister Mahar?" and I said, "No, I don't have a car, I walked over." At that point the audiologist came over and, since these people seemed to be having difficulty understanding simple sentences, I said, in a very loud voice, "I'M HERE FOR A HEARING TEST." In an equally loud voice she said, "I'VE GOT NEWS FOR YOU, YOU'VE FLUNKED ALREADY."

This really wasn't news to me because I'm always

flunking stuff. It really went downhill when they put the headphones on me and played various frequency squeals. How am I supposed to tell those from my regular squeals? Then, with her mouth covered so I can't see her lips, she recited a whole lot of words I'm supposed to repeat. How am I supposed to know what she is saying if I can't read her lips?

Well, I finally did get a hearing aid—the most powerful one they had. Now I can hear things I haven't heard for years. But it has its problems. One Saturday I took the whole furnace apart trying to find the chirpy noise only to discover it was a couple of robins outside the basement window. I can now hear what people are saying about me. But I miss my chimes; I miss playing charades; I don't like what people are saying about me. I think I'll turn the fool thing off.

Chapter 31
Darling, I Am Growing Older

I have finally reached, and passed, the Biblical allotment of three score years and ten. It took me over seventy years to do it, and there were more than a few times when I thought I wouldn't make it. Every day, from here onward, is a bonus that I accept with gratitude and will attempt to use wisely. Even a few years ago, I began making concessions to my advancing years. I now have a more thoughtful approach to the process of awakening each morning; no longer do I leap out of bed and madly rush to meet the day. Instead, there is a more calculated beginning that acknowledges life may not be quite as certain as once it seemed to be. There are four individual steps.

In step one, lie perfectly still. Give no indication that you are awake. With your eyes still closed, simply lie there and listen carefully. Above the steady hum, whine and whistle of your tinnitus, do you hear the splendid solemnity of a church service? Is there the subdued whispers of friends saying the only nice things they've said about you in years? Are relatives discussing your will, your insurance or lack thereof? If the answer is no to these questions, proceed to step two.

Still with your eyes closed, take a deep breath. Do you smell the pungent odour of incense? How about the aromatic fragrance of fresh-cut floral arrangements—particularly lilies? No? It's looking good—go to step three.

Open your eyes. Without moving your head, glance slowly around the room. Are there small groups of people in dark clothing? Do you see any tall, lit candles? Is your wife being consoled by someone you haven't seen in a decade and whose name you can't remember? If you can reply in the negative to these questions, you are all set to take the final step.

Sit up slowly and with great dignity on the side of the bed. Stay there for a few minutes. Remember—even though your blood is still circulating, it does not circulate very fast and it doesn't circulate everywhere. Be patient, give it a chance to catch up. If, after a few minutes, nothing seems to be aching worse than it did yesterday, and you appear to be in reasonably good shape for the condition you're in, smile and very quietly whisper—Hallelujah! You have been granted another one thousand four hundred and forty minutes. Get up and enjoy each and every one of them.

Please don't think that this cautious approach reflects the worry of an imminent demise on my part. Nothing could be further from the truth. I descend from a lineage that is noted for their longevity. Most of them lived to a ripe old age, and some made it to overripe. There is a story, handed down in my family, that in the village where they originated, three of my forebears had to be shot in order to start the local cemetery!

Anyone my age was considered a callow youth. At sixty-five, the age when most people retire, my Uncle Albert developed acne. He did not get whooping cough, measles or any of the other childhood illnesses until he was in his late eighties. Uncle Ed was another. In his late eighties he was still playing the violin in an all girl orchestra. At least that's what I think he was doing. Whenever I asked anyone where Uncle Ed was, they would say he was out fiddling around with a bunch of women. If he hadn't been murdered by a jealous husband when he was ninety-three, who knows how long he might have gone on enjoying his great love of music.

The shining example was, of course, my grandmother on my father's side of the family. The dear old soul was still an attractive, vivacious woman even after she passed the age of one hundred. She was interested in everything new and was very alert and active until the end. She died, suddenly, at the age of one hundred and three. She wouldn't have died then if her parachute had opened. Actually, the fall didn't kill her; the parachute had deployed enough to slow her down, and she was probably only going about sixty when she hit the runway. It did break her pelvis and both ankles. Being the proud old darling she was, she insisted on driving herself to the hospital. When they pried her Harley Davidson out of the gravel truck's grille, they found the speedometer jammed at ninety-eight miles per hour!

I hope to maintain the family tradition. The older I get, the older I want to be. I have always considered whatever age I am the best age to be—seventy is no exception. If they are going to call you a senior citizen at age fifty-five, then I have to be a senior senior and I am entitled to all the wonderful advantages of that designation.

Right off the bat I don't have to worry about dying young. I passed young so long ago that I hardly remember it. Even dying at middle age is not a concern. You would have to be a bigger optimist than I am to anticipate reaching 140.

At this age you finally command some respect. Twenty years ago nobody gave a hoot what you thought about anything. Now people listen to what you have to say; they figure if you have reached this age, are not drooling excessively and seem to be reasonably lucid, you must know something. They don't expect you to know how to operate a computer, program a VCR or use a microwave oven—when they find out you know more about it than they do, it comes as a culture shock and they regard you with awe.

The fact that you grew up in the same era as Charlie Chaplin, Greta Garbo, Mae West and W. C. Fields, the fact that you saw Babe Ruth and Lou Gehrig play baseball and you were around when Charles Lindbergh crossed the Atlantic, and you're still breathing, commands respect. You are living history. What they are calling history, you were calling current events. George Burns has mastered this art. When he walks out on stage, he gets a standing ovation, and all he's doing is breathing.

To keep this respect, all you have to do is keep on inhaling and exhaling. It's really that simple.

If there is something you don't want to do, pretend you don't hear them. Everyone expects you to be hard of hearing. If that doesn't work, mention your arthritis, bursitis or whatever '-itis' is acting up at the moment. If there is something heavy to be lifted, cough and rub your chest. They'll sit you down on a comfortable chair, give you a nice cup of hot tea and from there you can have an enjoyable time watching young people developing hernias.

You don't have to worry about long-term investments or products with a forty-year guarantee. You don't have a long term and the product may be guaranteed for forty years—but you're not. Even buying green bananas could be somewhat risky.

One of the biggest advantages is you have much less stress in your life. Almost all of the people that caused you stress are dead now; you went to their funerals years ago, maybe you even snickered a little. And the situations that caused you stress have been solved by someone else. No one gets alarmed if you still smoke a few cigarettes from time to time. By now you have smoked the equivalent of a cigarette about seventy miles long; how much harm can another few feet do?

No one expects you to do much in the way of exercise. They figure getting dressed in the morning pretty well handled it for the day.

Above all, you have reached the age where you know what is important and what is not. You can tell the real from the phoney; the worthy from the worthless. With a little bit of luck you may have many more days to enjoy that which is important and the willpower to say no to that which is not.

Chapter 32
Mixed Messages

I blame the total state of confusion in which I exist today on the mixed messages I got from older people in my early, formative years. When I was born I had two half-brothers; one was six years older and the other was older than me by eighteen years. From my very first memories both of them were always on my case. In effect I had three 'fathers.' The younger one was always saying, "You want to smarten up, kid," and the older one was always saying, "You want to smarten up, boy." Until the time I joined the air force, I thought my first name was "kid," my middle name was "boy" and I wasn't too sharp.

One of my earliest memories was the Great Parachute Caper. When I was ten, I saw a movie that showed the very latest craze, people jumping from aircraft with parachutes. I thought, "Wow! Isn't that wonderful; with one of those I could spend all summer floating through the air!" Well, I didn't have a parachute but I did 'borrow' my mother's umbrella. I know it's smaller than a parachute, but I was smaller than the man, so it should work. I was smart enough to make a trial jump from the garage roof (twelve feet high) before I tackled the really high stuff. The umbrella turned inside out, and I hit the ground with a terrible thud. The doctor said, "The lad didn't break anything except all existing records for stupidity." For the rest of the week I limped around listening to, "You better smarten up lad/boy/kid." Everyone failed to notice I was smart enough not to use Dad's umbrella.

One Sunday, in late summer of the same year, my mother said, "We are going to visit your Aunt Minnie, put on your new pants, a clean shirt and go out and play until we are ready. AND DON'T GET DIRTY!"

Those two sentences are completely incompatible. The only way I could stay clean was to stand in the middle of the yard wrapped in a blanket. I get bored easily. I decided to do some pole vaulting, that should be safe, after all you're up in the air part of the time and the air is clean, at least it was in those days. Things were going pretty good so I decided to vault over the picket fence. Unfortunately, there was a nail sticking up on one of the pickets. The three-corner rip in the seat of my pants did not seem insurmountable. I 'borrowed' a needle and some thread, hid in the bathroom and twisted my pants around and carefully stitched the rip. It looked okay—not great but okay. For the rest of the day I was a model child. Instead of roaring around the farm, chasing chickens, aggravating the horse and hunting for snakes, I sat quietly listening to the older people discuss who was dead, who was dying and what a mess the government was making of everything; conversations I still listen to from time to time to this very day. I was very polite and at no time did I turn my back on anyone.

Later that night, when I discovered I had sewn my pants to my shirttail and my shirttail to my underwear, I had to confess. My mother laughed so hard she forgot to get mad. I learned two lessons—always be born to parents who have a great sense of humour; and, if you are going to do something stupid, be sure it's something stupid that will make them laugh.

Even when I did something reasonably clever, it didn't help. All it did was earn a different type of message. Take the time one summer when there was a hole in the screen door. When my father came home to dinner, my mother was complaining about the flies in the house. Dad fixed the screen and then turned to me and said, "I have to go back to work, take the fly swatter and kill the flies; when I come home tonight, I'll give you a cent for every fly you've killed."

When he came home he said, "How many flies did you catch?" I proudly said, "I killed 137 flies." He screamed, "One hundred and thirty-seven—you killed 137 flies in the house?" I said, "No, I only killed eleven in the house; the rest were out by the garbage can in the back yard. I would have killed lots more but I broke the swatter."

He thought about it for a moment, "Okay, I'm a man of my word. I'll pay you the dollar thirty-seven, but in future I'll remember I'm dealing with a smart alec. From now on, don't get smart with me, son."

At least "son" seemed a step up from "lad," "boy" or "kid." But now I'm totally confused. What am I supposed to do? Smarten up or stupid down?

Chapter 33
We've Been Brainwashed

When I was in grade seven, we had to write a composition based on one of the five senses. I figured everyone else would pick the sense of sight or sound, so I decided to write about the sense of smell. I wrote about the smell of fresh, home-made bread, roses, lilacs, the smell of Christmas dinner in an old-fashioned kitchen and so on. I don't remember all of it, but I vividly remember my last sentence. Ever the comedian, my last words were, "And in conclusion, there is nothing I enjoy more than walking to the middle of a big field on a really hot day to just stand there and smell."

I don't think this composition started it, but up to that time there were only two types of soap. There were several varieties of white soap that were used for washing people and a yellow, lye soap that was used for washing everything else. Although a few times my mother used the lye soap on me when the people soap wouldn't work.

I suspect my composition was read by one of the soap manufacturers and this planted an idea—"Let's convince everyone they smell bad and they need our products."

Radio was in its infancy and this was the ideal medium to spread this propaganda. Someone came up with the brilliant idea of soap operas to captivate an audience, and the rest was history. The people who make toothpaste, deodorants and hair sprays, recognizing a good thing, jumped on the bandwagon. Later, with the advent of television, we were dead ducks. Television and radio has changed us into a bunch of neurotic nerds who are convinced that we have rotten teeth, bad breath, we smell awful, and without their products, we couldn't get through another day without offending everyone downwind.

I didn't realize how effective their brainwashing was until one night at the supermarket. My wife had asked me to pick up a special liquid soap to remove the soap-scum left by another liquid soap—a soap that is used to wash soap! How silly can it get? I stood in the soap section in awe. As far as the eye could see there were soaps. They had soap for dry skin, oily skin, sensitive skin and regular skin types. There were cake soaps, liquid soaps, powdered soaps, creamy soaps and even soaps that replaced the oil in your skin you had washed away with the other soaps.

The ultimate was a bar of soap with a loop of rope. You wore this around your neck while you were taking a shower. It was called "soap on a rope." It should have been called "soap for a dope." Anyone trying to wash their feet with that thing around their neck is going to break a leg—the rope isn't long enough!

On the other side of the same aisle are the deodorants, toothpastes, hair sprays and colognes. The deodorants alone run for approximately a quarter of a mile. You have many choices. You can smell like assorted flowers, old English leather, burnt rubber (for car buffs), or you can smell like nothing on earth if you use the unscented stuff. Personally, I never use the hair sprays or colognes but I enjoy being around people who do—they draw all the black flies and mosquitoes. This saves me the cost of repellents.

Toothpastes I don't even bother to give a glance. I've reached the age when I cannot only say, "Look, Ma! No cavities!" I can also say, "Look, Ma! No teeth!"

When I get to the section that has the adhesives for dentures, I notice there are still only two kinds. There's the powder that only holds till you drink the first cup of coffee and the paste kind that must be based on crazy glue—you can't get your dentures out for three days, and then you have to pry them loose with a screwdriver. There should be something in the middle. Maybe if they weren't busy inventing another zillion kinds of soap, they could find a powder adhesive where you're teeth popped out automatically after sixteen hours.

I'd like to apologize to everybody. I had no idea a simple, illiterate little composition on the joys of smelling by a twelve-year-old kid could cause this much trouble. Has anyone seen my bar of lye soap? I'd better wash up for dinner.

Chapter 34
The Funny Thing About Writing Humour

Last Saturday afternoon, when I was at the mall, a friend of mine said, with a perfectly straight face, "Did you hear about the guy in the car who ran over himself in the parking lot this morning?" Well, I hadn't heard anything about it and it sounded like a really weird accident so I said, "How did he do that?" With a smile of triumph, my friend said, "He stopped the car, rolled the window down and asked a couple of young kids to run over to the store and get a package for him. Both kids said no, so the man had to get out of the car and run over himself."

This silly story is possible because of the many meanings of the word "run." You can score a run in baseball or you can run a score with an orchestra. You can get a run in your stockings and a play may run for a year. If you run a specific distance in a competition, you can say you ran a run. You don't even need legs; you can run a business sitting at a desk. You don't even need to be a person; a train or bus can run from here to there and a machine can run without even moving anywhere.

The simple, little, three-letter word "run" has over eighty different meanings. Add an adverb and you can create hundreds more. Our famous "run over" has five meanings: 1. to ride or drive over something; 2. to overflow; 3. to go beyond a limit; 4. to examine or rehearse; and 5. to go from one place to another.

Even a word with only two meanings can be funny.

The word "handy" means (a) close at hand or nearby and (b) dexterous or skilful. Whenever one of our friends calls and wants to speak to my wife, they sometimes say, "Hello, Jim, is Rowena handy?" If I'm in a playful mood, and I usually am, my answer is, "No, but I'm going to keep her anyway—she looks really cute in front of the fireplace on a cold, stormy night." I took the second meaning.

At the beginning of this book I wrote a story, "The Sad Thing About Humour," in which I was deploring the limitations imposed on a humorist. Unlike the singer or dancer who can sing the same songs or dance the same steps every night, the humorist must constantly come up with new material. He or she cannot poke fun at ethnic groups, minorities, religion, mothers-in-law, wives, and a great many other subjects that would generate nasty letters and maybe even physical violence. Mark Twain once said, "There are several kinds of stories but only one difficult kind—the humorous." This is true, it takes a lot of sense to write good nonsense, but you are aided and abetted by a wonderful instrument called the English language. This is a language rich in oxymorons, words that can't be—there is no such thing as Charlie Brown's "good grief" or Juliet's "sweet sorrow" and something is either full or not, it can't be "fuller." Then there are synonyms, words which should mean the same but can be twisted. If someone tells you that "unlawful" and "illegal" mean the same thing, you can assure them they don't. Unlawful is anything that is against the law, and an illegal is a very sick bird. Try that on a law student.

Homonyms, words pronounced the same but with entirely different meanings, such as heir, ear, err and air can add to the fun. Thanks to the Reverend W. A. Spooner, famous for his "tips of the slung," we have an endless supply of "spoonerisms." Instead of a well-oiled bicycle, we can have a well-boiled icicle, or, instead of "stand back and let the coffin pass," we can "stand back and let the parson cough." Above all, there is just plain old-fashioned confusion. Many years ago, for the Department of Agriculture, I had to do an article on the cultivation and uses of blueberries.

For research, they gave me a guided tour of a blueberry farm, and I watched a huge spreader at work between the rows of bushes. "What is he putting on your blueberries?" I asked. My guide said, "It depends on soil conditions, in this particular field they are using a mixture of sheep manure and bone meal." With a straight face I answered, "Sounds interesting. I must try it; back home we've been using a mixture of cream and sugar on ours."